i Know
just how
you feel.

I Know Just How You Feel.

Cheryl Meier

THOMAS NELSON PUBLISHERS
Nashville • Atlanta • London • Vancouver

Published in Nashville, Tennessee, by Thomas Nelson, Inc., Publishers, and distributed in Canada by Word Communications, Ltd., Richmond, British Columbia.

Scripture quotations are from the NEW KING JAMES VERSION of the Holy Bible. Copyright © 1979, 1980, 1982, Thomas Nelson, Inc.

Scripture taken from the HOLY BIBLE, NEW INTERNATIONAL VERSION® are marked (NIV) in the text. Copyright © 1973, 1978, 1984 by International Bible Society. Used by permission of Zondervan Bible Publishers. All rights reserved.

Italics used in Scripture quotations are added by the author.

Library of Congress Cataloging-in-Publication Data

Meier, Cheryl.
    I know just how you feel / Cheryl Meier.
        p.   cm.
    "A Janet Thoma book."
    ISBN 0-8407-4399-8
    1. Teenagers—Prayer-books and devotions—English. 2. Devotional calendars.
I. Title.
BV4850.M45   1993
242'.63—dc20   93-44820
                                                                         CIP

Printed in the United States of America.
2 3 4 5 6 — 99 98 97 96 95

It is fools, they say, who learn by experience.
But since they do at last learn, let a fool bring his experience
into the common stock that wiser men may profit by it.

C. S. LEWIS

CONTENTS

A Word from a Dad

When I wrote *Don't Let Jerks Get the Best of You* and was vulnerable about much of my own jerkiness, my daughter, Cheryl, offered to add a chapter. I laughed and said, "Thanks but no thanks—I'd rather limit my exposure!"

So here she goes, instead, writing her own devotional and exposing our whole family for the world to see!

Call me a prejudiced father, but Cheryl has done an excellent job of articulating the pains and joys we all experience, growing through those awesome but difficult teen years. And she does this particularly well because she was a teenager when she wrote the book. Cheryl recognized that sometimes you want to talk to someone who is right where you are, someone who can relate to what you're feeling—now!

In *I Know Just How You Feel,* Cheryl talks openly and honestly about the challenges of her own teen years: dating; relating to her family; learning to be herself; learning to live a balanced life, committed to God while still being a part of the community. She relates her experiences and feelings to the readers' experiences and feelings, and she even gives a little insight into what it's like to be the daughter of a psychiatrist.

I heartily endorse *I Know Just How You Feel* for teens *and* for their parents.

I Never Read Introductions

I never read introductions to books, so you're free to skip this one if you want. I just wanted to tell you something about this book so you can see if it is right for you.

This is a devotional book written for teenagers *by* a teenager. (I'm in college right now, but I'm still in my teens.) I wrote it because I sometimes find it really difficult to relate to what adults are saying to me, and I think other people my age feel the same way. Sometimes we want to hear things, not from older people who have experienced it years ago, but from someone who is going through it right now.

I've got to tell you up front that I *don't* have all of the answers to life's problems. I don't even have the answers to all of my own problems! But in *I Know Just How You Feel*, I have tried to talk about some of my good times and some of my tough times. I hope you can relate to what I have experienced because I wrote this book for you. I never would have finished if I didn't think that someone out there might be going through what I've been through.

You can read this book straight through from chapter 1 to chapter 49. Or, if you'd prefer, you can skip around and find the chapters you can relate to best.

Every chapter ends with a Scripture verse, which relates to

that chapter. These verses have encouraged me through the years and will be the best source of guidance you will find here.

That's really all, except I hope this book will encourage you and help you. Most of all, I hope it will help you remember that you are not alone!

And the God of all grace, who called you to his eternal glory in Christ, after you have suffered a little while, will himself restore you and make you strong, firm and steadfast.

1 Peter 5:10 (NIV)

1

This Is
for You

I don't want to sound like the leading authority on life, because I'm not. The only reason I am writing this book is because I care about you.

I don't mean that superficially, nor am I saying it just to say it. I'm saying it because, even though I don't know you personally, I believe you are a lot like me.

Maybe you are wondering if you'll ever be "good enough" or if you'll ever find anyone to love you just as you are. Maybe you're wondering why everyone else's life seems so perfect. Or maybe you're wondering if you are ever going to stop running to drugs, to sports, to work, to school, to church, to friends, to TV, to music, to *anything* in order to avoid sitting in silence for a minute to see who God really is.

Have you gotten so sick of standing alone for what you believe in that you've started to think about compromising your values to take the pressure off? Or are you so sick of compromising that you don't know how to recover your values? Are you tired of falling for so many lies that you don't even know what the truth is, and you don't care anymore?

Are you tired of trying to live by a bunch of Christian "dos and don'ts" that you're tempted just to throw it all out? Maybe you are tired of feeling so out of control you think you're insane, or possibly you are tired of having such a "perfect" life that you wouldn't even know if there were something wrong.

Well, whether you're sick or tired or just wondering, I think I know how you feel. One thing I've learned is that if you ask God to make you more like Him, He will change your world. God does not mess around. He loves us and is gentle with us, but He also disciplines us, and a lot of the time he does it through the things that happen in our lives.

That's sort of what my life has been like the last few years. It felt almost as if God was saying to me, "Oh, hi Cheryl. No, you really should not date non-Christians. And by the way, I'm going to move you from Bible-belt Texas to liberal California. Oh, I see you're all alone. Why don't I put a good Christian friend in your life like you've been praying for. Oh, sorry; it's time for me to move your new friend to England. . . ."

Thanks, God!

No, I really do mean thanks now. I just didn't understand or want any of it at the time. I think that since I am such an extreme person, it sometimes takes extreme things for God to get through to me.

Anyway, I truly am writing this book for you. I really believe that God is working in your life for a purpose. I believe that He listens to you personally and knows your needs completely. In fact, I think He may have taken my closest friends out of my life right now so that I could take the time to reach out to you.

I pray for the best for you. God needs you here to do something unique that He is preparing you for. God will help us, and someday we'll have a closer friendship than the ones we have developed in these short years of life here on earth.

This is what the LORD says—
    he who made you, who formed you in the womb,
    and who will help you:

Do not be afraid. . . .
For the LORD comforts his people
    and will have compassion on his afflicted ones.
                    Isaiah 44:2; 49:13 (NIV)
                    44:1-5 ; 49:8-26

2

Being Real

Have you ever known people who always made a big point of wearing "name brand" clothes even though they couldn't really afford them? I have. I've also known some really wealthy people who liked to go around in old cutoff jeans and a T-shirt.

There are some people who wear big crosses and tell people about their long quiet times but who are really not close to God at all. And there are some Christians who are deeply committed to Christ and who show it in their lives, but they do not go around bragging about it or acting like they never have any struggles.

The point is, you can't always tell if someone is really a Christian just by looking on the outside. I have already mentioned how frustrated I get at some churches, Christian schools, and Christian camps because of all of the masks people wear. They seem to think they always have to act happy and spiritual and talk about how many people they witnessed to that day.

Well, one big problem I have with this kind of people is that when I'm around them I start thinking that something is wrong with me. I'm not like these "perfect" Christians, so maybe I'm following God the wrong way.

I know I'm not supposed to compare myself to other Christians. But realistically, I need to know what it looks like to live as Christ did, and the only way I know to do that is to follow someone's example. I find it confusing to try to live for God and to follow His Word when I feel I may be doing it all wrong.

So how can I know how to act as a real Christian? How can I be sure that I'm more than just a "name brand" Christian? Here's something that has really helped me sort this out: I ask myself, *Cheryl, is God at the center of your life, or is He just a part of your life?* If God is truly at the center of my life, then everything that happens to me and everything I do will reflect that. And when that's true, I'll be living a real Christian life.

If you are confused about what it means to put God at the center of your life, then maybe you can look at it this way. We need to continually put our focus on God, not on other people. Not on our pastors. Not on beautiful sunsets. Not on ourselves. When our attention is on serving God and on glorifying Him when we see His presence in others and in our surroundings, then our focus is right. But when our attention is on making ourselves look like better Christians and checking to see if others measure up to the outward standards, then our focus is off.

Putting God at the center of my life means that when I have a problem, my first response is to pray and to go to the Bible for an answer. It also means that when I don't make time for prayer and Bible reading, I miss my time with God.

It means that when I get mad and yell at someone, I think, *God, please forgive me. I am so weak. Thank You for using me and forgiving me in spite of how I am constantly messing up.*

And it means I can look at the sunset and one of my first thoughts is, *God, You are so beautiful!*

All these examples of internal decisions are between me and God. God does not judge by outward appearances. He looks at and weighs the heart. We are walking as Christians when Christ is living and growing inside of us and when He is our first priority.

Some Christians may think we're slackers or heathens because we don't act like they think we should. But God knows

exactly how we are inside. And if we are consistent in seeking Him, then people will eventually see the sincere love we have for God and our true desire to follow Him.

One more thing. I'm not saying that all people who are outgoing or happy about their faith are fakes. And I'm not saying that all people who don't talk about their faith are committed Christians. (That would be like saying that everyone who wears designer clothes is only pretending to be rich, and everyone who wears jeans and T-shirts is really rich.)

I guess I am being as judgmental as the "outward" Christians are when I accuse them of faking their Christianity because they display their faith. I have to remember that there are many different kinds of Christians who express themselves in different ways. God knows who the sincere ones are. But I think we will be a lot less confused and more at peace when we begin to be real with God, ourselves, and others!

Stop judging by mere appearances, and make a right judgment.

John 7:24 (NIV)

3

What's Best

$\mathcal{T}$hink of the last time your parents told you to do something, and you thought it was *totally* dumb. You did not understand why they wanted you to do it, and you knew your way was better.

Have you heard the line, "I just want what's best for you"? And did it really make you mad because their idea of "what's best" was not what you wanted to do?

One night I was at home talking on the phone to one of my friends. We both were really bored, so we wanted to do something together to have some fun. I asked my parents if they would drive me over to my friend's house, but they said no. I argued. They still said no. I was pretty mad. So then I said I would walk. We lived by this golf course, and it would be a long walk to Tami's house on the main road. But it was not far if you cut through the golf course.

Well, my parents did not like this walking idea at all. They said, "Cheryl, there is no way that we are going to let you walk across that golf course in the dark!" Well, I just thought they were being paranoid as usual. I mean, who would be on a golf course to "get me" at eight-thirty at night? So I grabbed my bag and left. Well, I got so scared on that dark golf course that I was practically running the whole way to Tami's—and I was not about to cross that golf course again on the way back. I don't remember how I got back home that night, but I am sure my parents do.

I do not really know what I was thinking to go out by myself on the golf course at night. I don't know why I thought I knew better than parents, except that I wanted to have a good time regardless of the risks I had to take or the people I would inconvenience.

I think we're that way with God a lot of the time. God made everything, so He really does know what's best for us. When we listen to Him, He shows us the truth. But sometimes the truth is hard for us to take because we don't really want to know what it is!

I know this guy who used to break into cars and steal them. He would strip off the leather seat covers and take out the radios, and then he would ditch the car on some street. When I met him, he hadn't done this in a long time. He was working at his job, and he finally saved up enough money to buy a car of his own.

One night he came by and we were talking, and I said to him, "Seth, what would you do if someone took your radio?" Wouldn't you get mad if someone stripped your car . . . everything you had saved up for? Seth said, "Of course I would get mad! This is my car. I worked for it." So I asked him why he used to steal other people's cars, and he said that was a lot different. He said he only stole cars from rich people who didn't deserve to have such nice cars—and besides, he needed the money!

We all try to rationalize our actions because we do not want to see or hear the truth. We think that as long as we are getting what we want, then nothing else matters. We don't want to stop and think, "Hmm, how would I feel if someone did this to me?" or, "How could this hurt me or someone else in the long run?"

I'm like that a lot. When I am doing something wrong or unhealthy or just dumb, I don't want to listen to God or my parents or anyone else. Somehow I convince myself that I know what's best and nobody else knows anything.

Realistically, what do you think is going through your parents' minds when they tell you no about something? Say, for instance, that they say you can't spend the night with a certain person. Do you really think they are saying to themselves, "Oh, great! Now is the perfect time for me to ruin Tracy's life. I don't want her to ever have any friends or fun. No, Tracy, you can't go and spend the night"?

Although it's easy sometimes to think that way, you know that is probably not true. There may be a lot of reasons why your parents did not want you to spend the night that night: (1) They knew you were sick and they didn't want your friend to get sick, nor did they want you to stay up all night and get even sicker. (2) They didn't know your friend or your friend's parents well enough for you to go over for the whole night. (3) They were planning to do something as a surprise for the whole family early the next morning. (4) They felt you had the whole year ahead of you and you could spend the night another weekend!

While there are exceptions, I think it's fair to say that most parents really do love their children. And most parents have been around at least twenty years longer than their teenagers have. That means they have been through a lot more than we have, so in many cases they *do* know best.

So if we can try to understand that our parents really do know more about some things—and even our older brothers and sisters know more about some things—why is it so hard to understand how much more God knows and how much He can help us?

Why do you think God asks us to give all our burdens and problems to Him? The Bible says it's because He cares for us! God is not in heaven yelling at us, like our coaches sometimes do, to follow all the rules and do exactly what He says right now. No, God is patient, loving, forgiving, full of grace and

understanding, always listening to us and thinking about us! And, unlike our parents, God is perfect. He's not subject to human sin and selfishness that get in the way of even the wisest, most loving parents.

Let's say, for example, that you want to go over to your best friend's house. Maybe her parents are going through a divorce and she really needs to talk; you're a little worried about her. So you ask your dad to take you over, and he says no because he's watching TV and doesn't want to get up and drive you.

Well, stuff like that has happened to most of us so many times sometimes it is hard to understand that God is not like that. God is not going to give us everything we want, but He is not selfish in any way. He does not care more about watching TV than talking to us. God is never too busy for us!

When I do not get what I want from God, it is because He always knows what is best for me . . . and He knows the right time to give it to me. What I have to do is trust Him enough to listen to the truth and follow Him.

> **Trust in the LORD with all your heart,**
> **And lean not on your own understanding;**
> **In all your ways acknowledge Him,**
> **And He shall direct your paths.**
> **Proverbs 3:5–6**

4

My Love Life in God's Sight

*I*s it ever going to happen?

I definitely do not think it is fair . . . it always happens this way! I start to like a guy, and I find out he's not a Christian. "See ya!" Then I start to like another guy who I know is a Christian, and he ends up ditching me for my best friend. Some other guy becomes interested in me (yea!), but for some reason I am just not attracted to him.

Okay, I move on. I meet the perfect, Christian guy at camp and like him for a month. And then we go back to high school . . . one thousand miles away from each other. Doesn't work again. God, are you trying to tell me something?

Okay, I'll wait till college. So I go to a Christian college thinking, "Oh yeah, here we go."

What?! Rumor has it that guys in this college don't date. Oh, great! Classroom after classroom full of Christian guys who aren't interested in girls—what's the deal?

Um, God, didn't you make Eve for Adam because you thought that Adam shouldn't be alone? Is it *wrong* to want a boyfriend?

Still no answer. Okay, I meet this guy who's a great Christian. I have known him for a while now. But I look at him, and he looks away. I talk to him, and he talks to me like I am a kid. What is the deal? Well, I am a freshman in college and he's been out of college for a year. Everyone tells him not to go out with younger women. So he finds out how old I am and then leaves to look for someone closer to his own age. Great!

What are you doing, God? Why did you make males and females? To torture us until the right time?

I'm trying to learn, God. I want to learn how to depend on You. I want to know in my head and heart that You are the only one who can make me complete and fill me with your love! God, change my heart. Help me to stop obsessing and thinking a guy will solve all my problems. Help me understand why you say that a woman should leave her father and mother and cleave to her husband, and that we should love You with all our hearts and love others as ourselves. Did you just mean our neighbors and our family? Did you not want me to ever learn how to love someone else and spend the rest of my life with him?

God, what is this "p" word that you keep throwing in my face? I don't want to learn patience in finding a relationship. Can't you teach me patience in school or something? Can you please help me *want* to be patient?

Lord God, I can't wait ten more years! Please show me what You want to show me *now!* Help me to see that you want what is best for me, and that You know what is best for me.

Lord, help me to desire Your will for my life and not my own. Lord God, I'll try to change my will . . . just show me how. I cannot do it without You.

Lord God, show me, please, the right thing to do!

And *please* take all of these stupid love songs off the radio!

Therefore the LORD will wait, that He may be gracious to you;
And therefore He will be exalted, that He may have mercy on you.
For the LORD is a God of justice;
Blessed are all those who wait for Him.

Isaiah 30:18

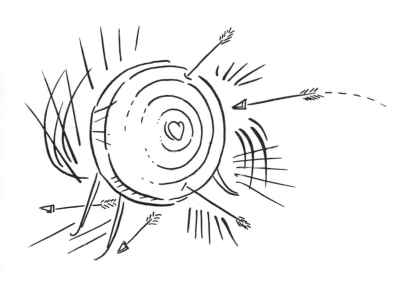

5

Growing Up
Is Hard to Do

Growing up isn't easy. Growing means change . . . and change can be really hard to deal with.

I mean, think about all the things that are happening to us as we try to get through this part of our lives. It is like no one can decide if we are children or adults. Sometimes people want us to be adultlike. ("It's time you showed some responsibility!") Sometimes they treat us like little kids. ("Why are you in such a hurry to grow up; you'll have plenty of time to drive.") And sometimes we're not even sure whether we want to be adults or go back to being little kids again.

You know what helps me understand this better? I think about a tree. (I know this example might sound "young," but sometimes the simple things show me so much.)

This is the idea: You and I, at our age, are kind of like little seeds that are in the process of growing into mature trees. Now, a tree seed might say, "But I like being a seed. Who wants to be a tree, anyway? They have to stand in the wind, the rain, the storms. And I could get hurt while I'm growing. What if someone climbs on me and breaks my branches? Doesn't sound like fun to me. I like lying here under this warm, comfortable earth with nothing in the world to worry about or to hurt me!"

But trees were not made to be seeds all their lives. And we

are not made to stay the same either. Growing up may be hard, but not growing up isn't an option either. Besides, there has to be something good about growing up.

While the tree grows from its little seed, it begins to see that, with God's help and protection, it can get through the storms. And as a grown tree, it can enjoy the warmth of the sunlight, the shade of the clouds, the refreshment of the rain, and the soft whisper of the breezes in its branches and leaves. It can know the satisfaction of providing a home for birds and animals and the pleasure of being with other trees.

As we grow, we can enjoy the freedom of making our own choices and living on our own. We can have the pleasure of seeing our futures open up before us and having our goals become reality. We can develop deeper relationships with people, possibly getting married and having a family. There are advantages to growing, even if it's painful a lot of the time.

But you may be one of those people who can't wait to be on your own. Adulthood isn't all that scary to you; it's just slow in coming! In that case, maybe you need to slow down a little. After all, as teenagers we are almost there.

What if a racehorse had a foal, and once it was six weeks old it was expected to run in a huge horse race with all the big, experienced horses? Don't you think it would get frustrated, upset, and hurt? Well, that is part of what would happen if we try to grow up faster than we are supposed to!

As we grow from infancy to childhood to being a teenager, we start to do more things for ourselves. We don't need Mommy or Daddy to feed us or dress us. And we start making more and more decisions on our own—what to wear, who our friends will be, how we spend our money. But we still need help from our friends, our parents, and others in order to grow.

Of course, we can (and do) learn a lot by ourselves by trial and error. But God gave us other people to help us and to save us some of the pain of growing up. He gave us parents. He gave us friends. He gave us preachers and teachers. If we help each other and listen to one another, things could go a lot smoother.

Growing up really is hard sometimes, but it helps to know that God is still in charge of the whole process. He wants us to move toward adulthood, but He is not going to push us too fast. He gives us different stages for a reason, so that we can grow in each part of our life.

We are like the tree that grows from a seed to a sprout to a sapling to a bigger tree with deep, strong roots; or like the foal that grows from a wobbly baby to a strong yearling to a powerful racehorse thundering down the track. Although the growing is painful at times, each stage of growth is designed by God to make us more complete and to give us a more fulfilling life!

He has made everything beautiful in its time. Also He has put eternity in their hearts.

Ecclesiastes 3:11

6

Pray?
What For?

god is so awesome! If you're not thinking that, then pray that God will show you His awesomeness!

It works for me. Today, for instance, God is showing me how faithful He is. No, nothing particular happened. I was just trying to sleep and I couldn't, so I started praying. I prayed for you, the person who's out there reading this book, that God would work in your life. I prayed that He would show me what you need to hear from a Christian sister. (That may sound dumb, but after all, we *are* going to spend eternity together!)

Then I started reflecting, thinking about how faithful God is. It is so cool to think about how God has a plan for you and for me.

I was also thinking that I wished there were a way I could hug Jesus. Then I thought of one of the girls in the junior high group I'm working with. I remembered her coming up and giving me a big hug. And I thought, *Janette is a Christian; Christ is in her. I can hug her every time I see her, and be hugging Jesus at the same time.*

I started praying for a shy boy in our group. I prayed that he would start depending on Christ to build him up, and that other Christians would reach out to him. Then I prayed that Craig would turn back to Christ and realize that God, our Father in heaven, won't leave him like his earthly father did.

I prayed for my best friend, and I thanked God for different people He has put in my life, including some non-Christians who have loved me and encouraged me more than some Christians have. I prayed that God will show them the truth somehow. I know that God hears me when I pray like that. He will lead my unsaved friends to the truth, and let them decide whether to accept it or not.

I just read tonight that God tells us to make the most of every opportunity. I want my non-Christian friends to be in heaven with us. I want your non-Christian friends to be there. You guys, we *can* make a difference.

When Peter said to pray without ceasing, I now know what he meant. There are so many things and people we can pray for. I hate wasting time, but when we pray we're never wasting time! God hears *every* prayer.

And it is fun to know that I can be here in Southern California at one o'clock in the morning praying for you, wherever you are whenever you read this. I can pray for my friends in Texas, whom I haven't seen for two years. I can pray for the baby inside my aunt's womb. I can pray for my dear friends and relatives in Arkansas. I can pray for my friend in Germany who is probably at work right now. I can pray for the man whom I someday will marry (if it's God's will). I can pray for my little sister whom I love and miss living with so much.

Prayer is *so* powerful. Jesus said that if we had faith as small as a mustard seed we could command the mountains to go into the sea and they would. James says that when we ask God for anything we must believe and not doubt. I'm not talking about a new red Porsche in the driveway. I'm talking about God's will. The Bible says God wants all people to be saved. So pray for unsaved friends and believe that God will show them what they need to know. Pray for people in need. Pray that God will give you and me the faith to believe, the will to pray, and the desire to pray. Pray that He will help us apply His work in our lives. And pray for other people who are reading this, too. We all need people to pray for God to work in our lives. God hears the prayers of a righteous person, and in Christ we are all made righteous.

We can pray for famous people, too. If they aren't Christians, we can pray they might see the truth and that they will never feel fulfilled without Christ. These people are very influential people. Let's all pray that someone will come along and show them Christ in a loving way, that someone will care about them enough to share the truth with them so that they can experience the Christian life and spend eternity in heaven.

And Christian people who are famous need major prayers. A lot of times I stop and pray for Christian singers, like Michael W. Smith and Amy Grant, that God will continue to work in their lives and help them and their families to keep depending on Him to meet their needs. In praying for them, I think how hard it would be sometimes to try to keep serving God when other Christians are lashing out and criticizing them.

I can't believe how lazy I can be sometimes. I can sit around and think, *Well, God's not putting anything in my life right now, so I'll just watch TV for a week.* But there are so many people I can pray for; I could seriously pray for a specific need of a different person every night for the rest of my life!

So please pray for me and I'll keep praying for you. We'll meet each other someday soon.

Pray without ceasing.

1 Thessalonians 5:17

7

Fake Christians

I'm walking on the grounds of a Christian camp, and I see smiling faces everywhere. None of the girls are wearing makeup, so it looks as if people are going to be real here. But that's not the way it turns out. Instead, people who don't even know me come up and ask me how my thirty-minute quiet time went this morning, which is very private. Other people come up to me and ask me how I am doing, but they aren't really interested in my response.

This has happened to me so many places—at church on Sunday, on weekend retreats, at Christian summer camps, and at Christian colleges and high schools. Why is it like this? What can I do?

I guess the world is like this, too. We're always expected to act like we're okay, not letting on if we're experiencing pain or unhappiness or grief. You can't go to school crying, or to work looking depressed, or to church showing deep pain in your eyes.

I get so sick of the way the world is! I run to my pillow in my room, lock the door, and talk to God. He is the only person I can be real with. He knows my heart, my thoughts, my fears, my pain—and He truly cares.

God does not record how long our quiet time was or how many people we talked to today. He wants you and me to

come to Him in all realness and let Him know what's going on in our lives. He doesn't want us to smile and say, "Oh, I'm doing just fine, thanks!" God is not like someone at camp or at school who thinks you are a drag or crazy if you say, "Well, I'm kind of depressed today." If we're not doing okay, God can deal with it.

People who feel they have to put on religious airs end up suffering more because they are ignoring all the sadness and anger they feel. How real do you think they are with God if they cannot even be real with themselves? How meaningful are their times alone in prayer or reading the Bible if they don't think there's anything wrong with them? How comforting are their relationships with other people if they can't share what's really bothering them?

Sometimes it's really hard for me to deal with Christians who act like that. I get really tired of carbon-copy Christians. I have to say that I have my own problems, yet God loves me where I am. So I need to love other people where they are. God works on different parts of our lives at different times. I want to be as real and honest as I can with them and still take my frustrations to God when others can't understand me and I can't understand them.

Avoiding superficial people is not the answer. We can learn more about God from all kinds of people. The problem for some Christians at churches and camps is they feel like they can't be themselves. If God can forgive our faults and still hang out with us, then surely we can love all Christians the way they are. Besides, when we start loving these Christians the way they are, they will have more freedom to be real.

Jesus . . . said to them, "Those who are well have no need of a physician, but those who are sick. I did not come to call the righteous, but sinners, to repentance."
Mark 2:17

8

What Does Your God Look Like?

When I moved from Texas to California a few year ago, people kept asking me if I rode a horse to school and if I lived on a ranch and square-danced to country music. Well, I laughed! I'm from Dallas, which is full of skyscrapers and billboards and traffic jams. So what could I do to help them find out what my life in Texas was really like?

I could tell them about how I never rode a horse in Texas and how tumbleweeds did not roll across the freeway near our house. And I didn't watch cows being rounded up! They could listen to me and understand and have faith that what I was saying was true, because I seemed to be honest with them about other things. Or I could get them a copy of *Texas Highways* magazine or the *Texas Almanac* and show them pictures of the city. Or they could go to Dallas and experience it for themselves. If they did all three, they'd really have a clear picture of where I was coming from.

And what's the point?

Just that some people's ideas about God are just as wrong as my California friends' ideas were about Texas.

Some people think that God is like a huge, white-haired judge ready to throw lightning down on all those who disappoint Him. Some people think He is a cuddly creature who just giggles and shakes a finger when someone does something evil. Some people think that God is a straitlaced Sunday school teacher who will not listen to you unless you are on your knees in a starched shirt or a white petticoat in a perfect white building with a cross on top. (Like God is really going to get mad if I don't wear nylons to church!)

It's a little like Santa Claus. Centuries ago, Saint Nicholas was a real person . . . a loving, giving person who changed many people's lives. Now, thanks to years of tradition, he is a fat, jolly man who goes down chimneys and rides in a sleigh pulled by a red-nosed reindeer.

Why do we believe what people tell us and live by old traditions? Why do we paint a picture of God in our minds that only partially reflects what He's really like? God has given us a perfect self-portrait in the Bible. He intended for us to read or hear His Word (the whole thing, not just isolated parts) and to think and to understand what He is like.

Nowhere in the Bible, for instance, does it say that God has declared that quiet times must be thirty minutes in length, that church should be no later than sunrise on Sunday morning, and that you can only talk to God about religious things, whatever those may be! Those are the kinds of ideas that come from old traditions and from other people's ideas of how things should work.

So where can people get a clear picture of God? It's like my telling Californians about Texas. We can (1) have a stereotyped image of God (usually acquired from radio, songs, friends, and other literature); (2) study the Bible to try to understand who God really is; (3) deny that there is a God and avoid having to deal with the whole mess (as my non-Christian friends would say!); or (4) look at Christians and see the ways that God works in them. Christians can also see God working firsthand in their own lives.

These ways of learning about God apply to Christians as well as to non-Christians. And some Christians can be just as ignorant about what God is like as non-Christians because so many Christians don't spend time thinking for themselves and studying the Scripture, or they do spend time listening to sermons of "religious" topics that don't have anything to do with Christ. (That's why Peter tells us, in 2 Peter 3:17, that we should always be on our guard for false teachers and not be carried away with what they say.)

What's the clear picture of God we'll get when we make use of all our sources to find out what He's like? This is the picture I get: God is not a God of white, middle-class, nicely dressed families. He is a God of all races, all colors, and all kinds of people: surfers, businessmen, motorcyclists, homemakers, punks, politicians, skaters, freaks, preppies, jocks—every kind of person. God has an open mind. He created *everything*. It's the people with closed minds, who are scared of people who are not like themselves, who do not think that God will listen to the prayers of someone with her nose pierced.

God sent Christ to die for everyone, and everyone who trusts in Him will go to heaven. We need to study God's Word and pay attention to how He works to get a clearer picture of who He is. Then we can show unconditional love to both the liberal Christians and to the legalistic Christians, because God's grace covers all of us who were called to Him!

But sanctify the Lord God in your hearts, and always be ready to give a defense to everyone who asks you a reason for the hope that is in you, with meekness and fear.

1 Peter 3:15

9

Hello, God; Are You There?

*L*ately it has been really difficult for me to believe that God hears my prayers.

Sure, anyone can say, "Cheryl, God loves you, listens to you, forgives you, and answers you," but that does not mean that those statements will immediately enter my head as facts! No matter how many times I hear the statements repeated, if I do not understand or cannot comprehend a little bit of how God loves me or when and why God does listen to me, then it is only information that will be stored in my head that will not make any difference in my life.

For this reason, I was thinking about prayer and wondering if there were some way that I could understand it better. My questions were probably a lot like yours: How can God hear me every time I talk to Him when everybody else is talking at the same time? Why doesn't God seem to answer me every time I pray? Am I doing something wrong? Doesn't He hear me? Doesn't He care? Why would God take time to listen to me when most of the people on earth will not? If God already knows my needs, then why should I tell Him? Why should I pray for my friends if I'm not even sure that God hears *my* prayers?

(No, I don't think it's wrong to express doubts like that! Most people have doubts, and facing them honestly pushes us to search for the answers and learn.)

Well, I decided that if I am going to spend any significant amount of time praying to the God I truly love and believe in, then I am going to spend some time thinking about what's really going on when I pray. And here's an idea that occurred to me.

Now, no analogy is exactly accurate, so please do not think that this is absolutely the way God hears and answers prayers. But this description helps me (and hopefully will help you) understand a little better how God works.

I thought, *What if God had an answering machine?* It would be like I pray to God on a direct line and talk to Him about everything. It is like God can somehow put the world on pause as He is getting my message, and He can listen to it completely and attentively and then write down (as if God needed to really write anything down) all of my needs, struggles, praises, thanks, hurts, and so on. My message reminds Him of what He already knows.

Then, I started to think about my earlier questions: Why isn't God answering me? Do I not matter? Did someone accidentally erase His messages? Does it take God a long time to get to my messages? Do my fears, tears, and requests not count? Is God screening my calls so that He does not have to answer me or talk to me? Did God forget my number? Does He think my messages are not important? Could his machine be broken?

Well, the truth, found in the Bible, is that God hears our requests, praises, and thanks before we even ask them, and He immediately decides what to do or not do about it. But a lot of the time what God decides to do is not what we think He should do. (What do we know about answering prayers; have we ever done it?)

Here's another thing I started thinking. There's always that one person on your answering machine who leaves about twenty messages compared to the one or two other messages you received. I think, *Do I annoy God when I keep calling Him and asking Him the same thing over and over again?*

The answer in Scripture is clearly no. Jesus told a parable about a widow who kept going back to the courthouse to ask for justice to be given to her. Finally, the non-Christian judge gave the widow the justice she was asking for not because he was being just, but because of her persistence in coming over and over again, and pleading for justice. Jesus explained that God will do much more than that non-Christian judge did for the widow because God genuinely cares about you.

Another example of persistence is the story of a blind man on the side of the road who yelled out over and over again, "Jesus, Son of David, have mercy upon me!" People tried to make him be quiet, but he persisted until Jesus came up to the man and asked him what his request was.

God is not deaf to our calling, nor are we drowned out by the calling of everybody else. Maybe God sees that if we keep asking Him over and over again then we are being sincere in our request and we are continually trusting that He will answer in His way when it is time. And sometimes, when I keep asking God for something, I eventually realize that either God has already answered my request (or is in the process of answering it), or that I really do not need that request answered in the first place.

I think knowing that the Holy Spirit intercedes for us and tells God our requests with words that we cannot express helps me understand that God hears my messages immediately and answers them, which causes me to want to praise Him and thank Him.

I think that I need to start going to God first about everything, because I know that He is going to answer me and not blow me off. He knows the best answer, and He has asked me to call Him and leave as many messages as I can!

If you are still hesitant about prayer, as I am sometimes, then try writing down briefly some of the messages that you have been giving God. In a month . . . or even a week . . . see how God has been changing you and your life and how He has been answering your messages!

Likewise the Spirit also helps in our weaknesses. For we do not know what we should pray for as we ought, but the Spirit Himself makes intercession for us with groanings which cannot be uttered.

Romans 8:26

10

God Always Knows

*I*t's the first week of chool. Kim walks through the student center and there is Michael sitting with several of her friends. They see her and wave. She walks over, and all the time she's amazed. She hasn't even thought about Michael for weeks now!

You see, last year Kim was really obsessed with Michael. She wanted to go out with him so badly; she just felt she needed him in her life.

Now, thinking back, she's a little embarrassed about liking him so much, although he never knew she was obsessed with him. She always wanted to know where he was, what he was doing, and who he was with. She tried as hard as she could to be where he was because she wanted to get to know him better. She was always nice to him, but was not overwhelming. It took so much self-control for her to back off and play everything cool, because her feelings seemed so strong.

All last semester she was on an emotional roller coaster. He would say something and she'd think, *Oh, he likes me,* and she'd feel great all day. Or he'd say something else, and she'd be torn to pieces because she thought he didn't like her. Then she would tell herself she never wanted to see him again; she kept looking for all of the bad things in him and was putting him down in her mind. She was angry at him and at God, too.

Why would God put this guy in her face just to tantalize and torture her? "What is wrong with me, God?"

She was so mad and frustrated that her whole personality changed for a while. She even started to think her parents and friends didn't love her much. She was depending on this one person to fill her loneliness. And since they never actually dated, she was pretty lonely most of the time.

Well, that semester of school ended. And now she realizes that this guy she thought she'd never get over has faded from her mind. Over the summer she matured in a lot of ways. She didn't even realize she had forgotten Michael until now when he waved to her across the student center.

She now reflects with amazement, *I don't even think twice about him! I still like him, but I don't feel this burning need for him in my life. I can talk to him without analyzing all his words over and over in my head. Instead, I can just listen and enjoy his company. This really is great! With or without Michael, my life will go on. I feel content, like God is in control. (He is in control!)*

If God ever wants this to work out, then it will. If He doesn't, then I know there are other guys out there. When and if the time is right, God will help me to find the right one. God always seems to know what's best for me.

"For I know the plans I have for you," declares the LORD, "plans to prosper you and not to harm you, plans to give you hope and a future."

Jeremiah 29:11 (NIV)

11

Read the Directions

ave you ever gone on a road trip with your family? Have you ever gotten *lost* on a road trip with your family?

Just think how crazy it would be if you wanted to get from Los Angeles, California, to Dallas, Texas, but you had no map or directions!

Or what if you wanted to bake a cake, but you had never cooked before and you had no recipe? How would you manage with no directions, no list of ingredients, and no idea how long to cook it?

Don't you think life would be a lot harder without directions of any kind? Well, God has given us clear directions about how to live, plus encouragement, in His Word. He has given us the message of His great love and forgiveness for every one of His children—that is, me and you. He has supplied us with everything we need to know in order to live in His love.

But this is not strictly a follow-the-directions, do-it-yourself situation. God did not give us His Word so that we can work our way into heaven. He knew that on our own we don't have what it takes! There is no way we can be "good" enough to get into heaven, even if we follow His instructions to the letter. No matter how hard we try, we would still mess up somewhere. You might obey your parents, but then tell your sister

you hate her. You might go to church all the time, but then be judgmental toward all the people who don't.

God knows we can't be good enough for His kingdom—no human being can. That is why He gave us *more* than a set of directions. He sent His only Son to live on earth as a human to show us how to live a life of truth. It is much easier, for me at least, to understand how to live correctly by seeing the way Jesus lived.

But even having Jesus' example doesn't guarantee we will never mess up. (You can follow the directions for baking a cake and still have the cake turn out wrong.) God allows natural consequences. If we are doing something wrong, then He will point it out to us. But in Christ, He also gives us a chance to repent, receive forgiveness, and then try again. That means we don't have to go around scared that we're going to do something wrong. We probably *will*, but we can come to Christ for forgiveness and then try again.

It's always our choice whether we follow the directions for driving somewhere or for baking a cake. And it's always our choice to accept what God has done for us in Jesus. God wants everyone to come to heaven, but He is not going to make us do anything! He gives us the freedom to choose to believe that Jesus died on the cross and rose from the dead three days later to pay for our sins. He also gives us the choice to read His written directions and to learn from them.

Now may the Lord direct your hearts into the love of God and into the patience of Christ.
2 Thessalonians 3:5

12

Cold
or Hot?

What would you do if you had a friend named Bartholomew? (Well, naturally you would call him Bart, but that is beside the point.) Let's say that you and Bart plan to go to the mall, but at the last second Bart decides that he doesn't feel like going. Then, you and Bart plan to eat lunch together, but when you go to the table to meet him he doesn't show up. And this isn't the first time it's happened!

You care a lot about Bart, and you forgive him, but then you find out that some other things are going on. For instance, he tells you that you are his friend, but he'll only admit that to the people at school who also like you. But for the majority of people who ask him if he knows you he would try to avoid the question, or he would simply say that he had no idea who you were.

Now, look, you are not dumb. Don't you think that by now you would be catching on to Bart's way of being a friend to you? If Bart were here right now, what do you think you would say to him?

Probably something like, "Look man, I really do like you, and I mean it, but I am getting tired of this. Are you my friend or aren't you? Do you want to spend time with me or not? Why do you keep telling people that you do not know who I am? I really get hurt when you bail out of half the plans we make.

Bart, I have forgiven you for everything that you have done to hurt me, but your actions are making it pretty clear that you really do not want to be my friend."

The problem with someone like Bart is that you cannot have a relationship with him because you don't know where you stand. He says he's your friend, but you can't talk to him because he's not honest with you. What he says and what he does just don't match. So you don't know whether he's your friend or not.

Now, how do you think God feels when we act that way toward Him? How do you think He feels when He's done so much for us, but then we only spend time with Him when we feel like it? How do you think He feels when we deny His name, or even curse His name in front of our nonbelieving friends? How do you think he feels when we don't make time to study the Bible?

Can you see why God hates it when we only pay attention to Him when we feel like it? Who wouldn't? That's why God tells us in Revelation that He would rather have us cold or hot, but not lukewarm.

God loves us and is committed to us so much that He sent Jesus, who is God, to be a servant here on earth. Jesus walked around telling people the truth, and then He died and rose again to prove that there is life after death and victory over sin. God loves us and will forgive us for everything if we let Him. And He would much rather have us say honestly, "No, I do not believe or accept Jesus," rather than to say "Sure, I believe in God," but not care very much for Him.

However, I don't think that wanting us to be cold or hot means God wants us to be unbalanced fanatics. I got a little carried away when I first understood what it meant to have Christ in my life. I wanted to be a strong Christian and avoid being lukewarm, but I didn't know what that meant. So I just

decided everything was wrong except for the Bible, church, and three basic meals a day.

Now, that is really limiting God! I mean, even Jesus went to parties. He told us to go out and be salt and light to the people around us, but to do that you have to get to know people in the world.

I've had to learn how to be more balanced. And don't think that I am the supreme expert on a balanced life, because God is *definitely* still working on me. But that's the best news of all. God wants us to be honest with ourselves and with Him. Once we do, whether we're hot or cold, He'll keep on working with us.

I know your works, that you are neither cold nor hot. I could wish you were cold or hot. So then, because you are lukewarm, and neither cold nor hot, I will vomit you out of My mouth. . . . Therefore be zealous and repent.

Revelation 3:15–16, 19

13

Are You God?

"Are you God?"

My brother Dan made me so mad when he asked me this question one day.

"Of course I am not God, Dan. Why would you even think that?"

He told me why. So now I am asking you, "Are you God? Do you think you are?" It's not as ridiculous a question as it sounds. After all, what do we do when we sin? We are saying, "I'm going to do it my way, not God's way."

I am not talking about those times when it's really not clear what's right to do. I am talking about the times when deep down we *know* that what we're doing is wrong . . . like telling our parents to shut up or signing their names so we can skip a class. By doing this we decide (consciously or unconsciously) we want to do it. And when we do that, we are saying that our ways are better than God's way.

How dumb can we get? After all, the Scriptures say that God at His most foolish point is wiser than the wisest person at his or her wisest point. Who are we to think our ways could possibly be better?

Why do we choose to sin? Because we are foolish and prideful. (I say *we* because I know how foolish and prideful *I* am.) Pride simply means assuming that I know better than God and/or anybody else. And again, that's just dumb.

Now, it's easy to take this the wrong way. I don't mean we

should go around with our heads down telling everyone how horrible and unworthy we are. That's a lie. God made each one of us and loves each of us. If we pay attention to what He says to us, we should feel important, desired, and valuable; and we should value others, too. We should not, however, think of ourselves as smarter or more important than God who created us. As Isaiah said, that would truly be like the pot or the clay saying they are more creative and wiser than the potter who formed them.

Now, if you ever meet anyone who has been my friend, I am ashamed to say that he or she can easily tell you how prideful and foolish I have been at times. I used to always go around pointing my finger at others who didn't behave exactly the way I thought they should—by going to "serious" Bible studies or by listening to my style of music. I wouldn't forgive my parents, friends, teachers, or pastors for slipping up. I wouldn't forgive myself either. I thought I was being such a good Christian by being miserable all the time and punishing myself for all the sins I had committed.

I assumed I did not deserve God's forgiveness. And that is true; none of us deserves it. It is a *gift.* But I would not allow God to forgive me, and I would not forgive myself.

That is why my brother was asking me, "Are you God, Cheryl?" I thought I was being such a good Christian by trying to follow every law and being terribly angry at myself whenever I messed up. I was very aware of how terrible my sin was and how foolish I was to do it. But I was being far more prideful and foolish to hold on to my guilt.

So please learn from my pain and my pride. If you have taken advantage of someone, hit someone, gone too far sexually, whatever . . . take it to God now. Confess it to Him and let Him forgive you. He can! No matter what you have done, or how many times you are reminded of it, take it to God.

You are not going to become more humble (as so many people incorrectly believe) by holding on to your shame and torturing yourself. The true way to learn how to be humble is to confess your sins honestly (no matter how ugly they are), ask God to forgive and heal you, then accept His forgiveness. Once you begin to realize how much God can forgive, you will also learn to forgive yourself. Then you will find true humility and experience the true love of God.

Woe to him who strives with his Maker! . . .
Shall the clay say to him who forms it, "What are you
making?"
Or shall your handiwork say, "He has no hands"? . . .
Thus says the LORD . . .
I have made the earth,
And created man on it.

Isaiah 45:9, 11, 12

14

Music

You've probably heard it before: "Burn those secular tapes!" (If you haven't, keep hanging around Christian circles, and you will.)

Okay, so we burn our tapes. Should we also burn all our books, dictionaries, and our clothes if they are not made directly by Christians? Should we not eat food at a certain restaurant because Christians did not prepare it? Should we not go to museums and see the beautiful paintings because Christians did not paint them?

Can you tell this subject frustrates me?

But wait a minute; I didn't always feel this way. Ask the people I hung out with in the tenth grade. Believe me, they remember. I would not even ride in the car with them because I did not want to listen to the secular music on the radio. But now I think I have a more balanced perspective. So let me throw out some observations from my experiences with music. Maybe they can help you think through your opinion of the music you listen to and the videos you watch on MTV.

Let's start with the fact that I am a Christian. Hopefully, you are too. And let's agree that a majority of the people who sing secular music are not Christians. Now, if these artists are not Christians, then their ultimate goal in life is going to be extremely different from yours or mine. I want to glorify God in all my thoughts and actions. They want to find something to fill the empty hole in their lives—and again, I am not at all

putting them down for desiring that, because God put that desire in all of us.

I really do not believe that all secular artists are trying to corrupt the minds of all the teens in the world. I do not think that all heavy metal bands want you to worship Satan. I *do* think, however, that these artists sing about the way they see life. So if one singer thinks it is okay, or even desirable, to sleep with lots of people, then she is probably going to sing about it. If a group thinks that they are possessed by Satan, then they are probably going to sing about it. If another band thinks that drugs are a good escape, then they might write a song about it. We are living in a fallen, sinful world, so people just sing about what they perceive to be the truth.

Okay, let's agree on something else. Anything we listen to over and over will eventually start to get inside our heads and influence the way we think. That's basic psychology. Repeat something enough times and we start to get used to it. (Madonna has said her goal is to keep exposing sexual messages so that the younger generations will be desensitized.)

Now, think about this. If we read the Bible, say fifteen minutes a day, and we listen to music three to six hours a day every day for years, which do you think will influence you more? If we read the truth which says "Do not be sexually immoral" fifteen minutes a day and we hear songs all day that say "Everyone is having sex, so go find someone and have your fun," then what are we going to think is true?

I agree with you that there are many songs about how ignorant prejudice is or about loneliness or about losing someone you love. There are songs by secular artists that have brought me closer to God than some songs by Christian artists. But over all, there are lots of songs that pull us further from God rather than drawing us closer to Him.

Of course, we have to take into consideration the quality of the music. A singer on MTV may project a wrong message and still be extremely talented. On the other hand, I can be in love with God and sing about it, yet my voice would not be considered talented. You may tend to thank God more for the vocal range of a talented singer than for any words that I croak out, no matter how meaningful they are.

But those aren't your only options. There really are many talented Christian soloists and groups, and I promise not all Christian music is "elevator music." If you haven't explored what's available, I urge you to give good Christian music a chance.

What you listen to is (hopefully) your choice. There's no need to be paranoid by seeing temptation and conspiracy in every radio and CD player. Just think about what you are hearing and how it might be distorting your thoughts and actions or how it is making the truth more clear.

I know, for me, that if I wanted to lie to someone it would be a lot easier for me to lie if I listened to songs saying that everybody lies and that's what I should do. I know a lot of times I feel like I am the only person in the world struggling with being a Christian. When I put in a Christian tape, it helps me realize that God is with me, and there are other Christians who believe the truth.

Again, it's your choice—just think about it.

It is better to hear the rebuke of the wise than for a man to hear the song of fools.

Ecclesiastes 7:5

15

Don't Judge a Book by Its Cover

Sometimes I feel like a book on a shelf
Standing alone, I am all by myself.
People walk by to just pick me up and use me . . .
Or just throw me down and hit or abuse me.
Their cares are my cover, or eye-catching title,
My contents and pages to them are not vital.
They couldn't care less if I'm torn deep inside . . .
Just stroll right by with a strut or a stride.
I want to just scream to let it all out
I wish they could see what I'm really about.
I wouldn't care who is dumb or who's smart.
I would open to each with all of my heart.

Why is our world so hung up on appearances? Why do we insist on judging people by their "covers" and never bother to find out what they're really about?

Why do we raise our noses when we pass by someone who is dressed wrong? Why do we ignore someone's answer to a question because of the way she talks? Why do we pretend not to see the guy with the glasses and the pocket protector? Why are we so insecure about ourselves that we have to make an outcast of anyone who is different?

First Samuel 16:7 says that God does not judge by outward

appearance; He looks at the heart. Why can't we learn to do the same thing?

It seems so ridiculous that people will shun some guy because he is "too tall" or "too skinny" or "too short" or "not muscular enough"—but it happens a lot. And girls are discarded because they're "too flat," "too tall," "too chubby," "too skinny."

This kind of judgment happens at school and at church. It influences our decisions on who gets to join clubs, who gets to be a cheerleader or the class president. But it gets really bad when we start looking for people to date or even to marry.

I may be prejudiced here, but I see it happen more with guys than with girls. I know, you guys are more visually oriented, and I can't completely understand that. But if you base your opinion of a girl's value solely on the way she looks, you are being deceived. There are tons of women who can get operations, starve themselves, get their hair dyed, and so on. Good-looking women aren't that hard to find! But it can be *very* difficult to find a woman who truly has a heart for God. You cannot go out and buy one of those. If you pass up a girl because she does not fit your blonde-haired, blue-eyed, perfect mold, then you may end up the loser.

But women do this too! If we are passing guys off just because they do not work out enough or because they cannot gain weight or because they have a crazy-looking haircut, then we're not only being shallow and superficial, but we may be missing out on someone great.

I'm tired of seeing it happen. I am tired of catching myself doing it, and I am tired of having others do it to me. If appearances are what we value in others, then we might as well give up on human beings and spend our time playing with Barbie™ and Ken™ dolls! If we only love at surface level, we'll always have a loneliness inside because we'll never learn to connect with others on a deeper level.

I'm not just talking about the way we judge others. Learning to love also means learning to accept *ourselves* just as we are. To value our "contents" as well as our "cover" and work to be beautiful on the inside as well as on the outside.

After all, the person inside is the person God loves. And He judges our lives by the book, not by the cover!

**Charm is deceitful and beauty is passing,
But a woman [or a man] who fears the LORD, she [he]
shall be praised.**

Proverbs 31:30

16

Praise God? Why?

*I*f you spend any time at all around Christians, you're going to hear something about "humbling yourself before God" and "praising Him." It's something Christians are supposed to do. But did you ever stop to wonder *why* we're supposed to do it? Do we think God needs for us to grovel in front of Him and give Him compliments to boost His ego?

The more I think about it, the more I think that humbling ourselves and praising Him is something we do for *our* sakes as well as His. It's a way of keeping us clear about who we are.

A child who is never taught to say thank you when she receives something will assume she *deserves* the gift. A child's mom comes to give her baby some milk, and the child assumes he deserves the milk. All his life he's gotten milk whenever he screamed for it.

And that's all right for little children; that's the way things are supposed to be. Eventually, though, for their own sakes, children have to learn to say thank you. And not just to say the words, which is always taught first, but to appreciate what is given and to realize the meaning of a gift. Otherwise they will grow up thinking they are the center of the universe.

This answers my own question about why I need to humble myself before God and praise Him. It means coming to realize

that a lot of times I am just like that child. And you probably are, too. We think we deserve our parents, deserve our good health, deserve our good churches, and deserve our homes. We think we deserve the luxuries of restaurants, good movies, TV, and other entertainment. Some of us even think we deserve the gift of life, so we think we have the right to kill ourselves if we want to!

Humbling ourselves before God is not a complicated theological idea that's hard to understand. It means getting it through our heads that we are God's creation and that our lives are a gift from Him that we do not deserve. This includes everything—the clouds in a clear blue sky, a rose in bloom, a close friend, a bully brother, and even final exams!

If you are like I am sometimes, then maybe we should both sit down for a while and think about this. Do we ever say thank you for the music we love, for the friends we have, for the beauty of God's world, or even for a toilet that flushes? Praising God should come naturally if we keep in mind that we are His creation.

Now, please, I'm not one of those Christians who bounces around saying, "Oh, hi; life is just grand and God is doing such wonderful things in my life." My life really hurts a lot of the time. But knowing that God is in control and that He deserves praise and thanks really does help me to get things in perspective.

> **He has shown you, O man, what is good;**
> **And what does the LORD require of you**
> **But to do justly,**
> **To love mercy,**
> **And to walk humbly with your God?**
>
> **Micah 6:8**

17

More Than a Grade

$\mathcal{L}$evi is sitting in class, and his mind is a million miles away. He doesn't like chemistry, and the teacher is a jerk. He's got so many other things he'd rather be doing . . . like skateboarding or practicing for the play or just hanging out.

Jessica is in church, squeezed between her mother and a little kid who keeps kicking the seat. It's hot and she's kind of mad at her parents for making her sit with them instead of with her friends. So she shuts down and sulks, not paying attention to what the pastor is saying.

Taylor's aunt buys her a teen devotional. She kind of glances through it, but doesn't bother to read it. So she just leaves it on her bedside table.

It's taken me a *long* time to get this through my head. Going to school does not make you intelligent. Going to church does not make you godly. Reading a book does not change your thinking patterns. You won't learn from any of these things unless you *want* to learn. But if you do want to learn, you can gain knowledge even from the lamest, most worthless class or sermon or book.

Take this devotional, for instance. Even if you do not learn from anything I say, you can at least learn for yourself how crazy it is for a teenager to try to write a book at all! Or you can learn from the verses. I mean it. If you do not learn and grow from the verses, then that is your choice—and you are free to make it.

Teachers have the hardest time these days because they have to motivate us to learn and then teach us at the same time. Now, I realize that none of us says, "I want to be stupid." But when I am sleeping on my desk, that is exactly what I am telling my teacher. When I act excited in class and just write down answers that I know my teacher wants to hear, then I am not learning anything but flattery.

I know that we all may get tired sometimes and turn off our brains, but it really gets to be scary if it becomes a habit. A lot of times people start thinking: *I go to school, so I must be smart.* Or they think, *Why bother with actually reading the assignments and doing the homework if I can pass without doing all those things?* Well, I think it is good to be motivated enough to choose to go to school, but it's such a waste of time if you are not learning anything! Learning is a lot more than just getting a good grade or graduating.

No one can really force us to listen and to understand; it has to be a choice that we make. I know some subjects seem so boring and pointless, and they're not always taught in the most entertaining way. But if you look for things to learn you will find them. It's true that it's easier to get good grades in the classes that interest you. I know for some people it seems impossible to be interested in chemistry, but for others it seems impossible not to be! And you cannot change your interests or your attractions a lot, but being interested in learning itself will help you to be interested in any subject. Learning something is always going to help you in the end.

The Scriptures say that every person gets a return for his labor (1 Cor. 3:8) and that whatever we do we should do it heartily for the Lord and not just to impress others (Col. 3:23).

If you work hard in school, then you will learn how to learn, and that will help you think more clearly in the long run. If you decide not to think about anything your teachers in school or your pastors at church tell you, then you are going to be wasting time for the next five to ten years. If you do not learn now to interact with your reading, your teachers, or your classes, then it is going to be a lot more difficult for you to be productive in the world when you have to earn a living, vote, and interact with others.

Katie had to learn the hard way. She had learned really early in school what it takes to get by; she sailed through high school by reading *Cliff's Notes* and occasionally cramming for exams. Then she went to college and failed almost every class her first semester. When she did try to study she had a hard time organizing the material, concentrating for long periods of time, or memorizing anything because she had never developed those study skills. Besides, all the material was unfamiliar to her because she never paid attention to it in high school. She would get so frustrated with herself because she was working so hard and not getting anywhere.

Katie was also going to church with some of her new college friends, and the pastor seemed to be saying some things she had never heard or thought about before. Could this new teaching be true? Katie had never spent enough time studying the Bible to be sure. She was finally put in a position where she was forced to think and make decisions for herself—and she didn't know how.

Katie decided that she really wanted to learn. She took a remedial study skills class and started spending more time with her homework and her Bible study. She's doing a lot better, but she's still mad at herself for wasting so much time.

May I remind you that I am in school right now; I am not an adult who has been out of school for years and has forgotten the mental torture that we all face sometimes! But I am learning that I only have myself to blame if I don't learn from school. What I put into school is what I am going to get out of it. And if I am not being challenged, it's up to me to challenge myself!

And whatever you do, do it heartily, as to the Lord and not to men.

Colossians 3:23

18

What's Up?

Emily knew everyone in her junior high. She was friendly and well liked by her friends. She was involved with three different sports and four school clubs. She loved being in ninth grade because she was familiar with the building, the teachers, and everything else at McKinley Junior High.

Then Emily entered high school, and she wasn't prepared for the huge change. Now she entered a cafeteria filled with hundreds of unfamiliar faces. She felt grateful when she saw one or two people she knew in the hall as she was running to her next class. She was not in any clubs or on any teams—she couldn't even find her way around the main building!

Every day for a week, Emily went home in tears and she didn't know why. She felt disoriented and confused. She would ask God, *What's going on? Why am I here? I used to feel so secure, but now I feel like no one knows me or cares that I'm here. I've got to go to this high school for three years . . . am I ever going to get used to it? God, do you have a plan for me?*

Going somewhere completely new—a new neighborhood, a new school, a new city—can be scary because it forces you to look at yourself without all of your friends, clubs, or sports. Suddenly it seems like your whole life is thrown up in the air, and you wonder if God is still beside you. Going to college can be especially hard as you leave all the people you are familiar with and move into a little dorm room with a total stranger. It

is easy in these insecure times to lose focus and grab on to whatever offers you a sense of comfort and belonging, including watching soap operas all afternoon, going out with any person who seems interested, or getting drunk at parties.

You know, it is so easy in life's confusing times for people to say, "Just have faith and God will bring you through." I've said it. You've probably said it at one time or another But like most truths, that one is a lot more difficult to live out than it is to say.

We can be so stubborn sometimes. I mean, the Bible is full of verses telling us that God knows and loves each one of us personally. He knows when one sparrow dies out of all of the birds in the world, and we mean a whole lot more to Him than a sparrow. He even knows the number of hairs on our heads. And He ought to. After all, He was there at the very beginning of our lives. He formed each one of us in our mothers' wombs, designed each of us individually and gave us our own free will. He also gave His only Son to save us from our sins.

When I sit back and look at everything God has written in His Word, it's obvious that I cannot begin to measure how much He loves me, guides me, and teaches me. So why do I feel so confused so much of the time? I think it's because I'm human. I do not know the ways of God, and I forget how much He loves me and keep insisting on my own way.

When I first arrived at college, I did not even know if it was right for me to be here. I did not know what I wanted to do with my life. I did not know a lot about myself . . . about who I was away from my familiar surroundings. Sometimes I would just yell at God because I was so mad and depressed that He was not sending me carved stones with my future written on them. When I met someone, I wanted to know exactly what would happen with our relationship. When God did not give me those answers, I practically fell apart. I could not handle all of the freedom that God was giving me.

I still do not have all the answers to make everyone feel

secure in their confusing times, not even for myself. But I know that God has not left me no matter how I may feel. He has promised that He will not leave, and He does not lie. I think, for me, God had to teach me to believe that He was there.

God sees me. He sees you, right now, reading this page. And when we ask Him to show us where He wants us to go and why we're here, He will eventually do it. He shows me what He thinks is enough for me to know that day!

Once we realize that God is in control of all things and thinks about each of us more than we can imagine, we can live a fuller life because we rest in His hands, trusting Him to show us piece after piece of our personal puzzle.

A man's heart plans his way,
But the LORD directs his steps.

Proverbs 16:9

19

Ethan at the Underground

*E*than could not believe what he was seeing. He had thought that drugs were so far away from his world, but there they were right in front of him!

Ethan had been going with a few of his Christian friends to different dance clubs (not the "pickup joints"). He had started loving the music because there were all sorts of beats and weird melodies . . . there weren't any "cheesy" lyrics about sex. Well, one night a couple of non-Christian friends had asked Ethan to go to a warehouse party. So Ethan and one of his Christian friends had decided they would see what it was all about.

Well, the music was great and wild paintings were hanging on the walls. Freaky films flashed on the ceilings and walls— stuff like *Willy Wonka and the Chocolate Factory* in fast motion and *King Kong* mixed with *Bugs Bunny*. It was really neat, except everywhere Ethan looked he saw people on LSD (acid) or taking the drug Ecstasy. Somebody offered him drugs as he came in the door. He went into the bathroom and three guys were trading multicolored pills.

Ethan felt so naïve. He had not thought that people took drugs very much anymore, especially after the "Just Say No!" campaign. (Wake up, Ethan!)

Ethan joined his friends who were dancing near the speakers. Some girls walked up, and Ethan recognized one of them; he had seen her at another club. She always wore a cross, so Ethan thought she might be a Christian. Well, she couldn't stop dancing, and she had an unfamiliar look in her eyes. Ethan asked her if she was on something, and she said, "Yeah, X." He couldn't believe it. He felt so dumb to think that just because this girl seemed nice and wore a cross, she wouldn't be on drugs.

Ethan found a dark corner and sat down to think. What was going on? The lighted warehouse seemed full of people having a great time—was he missing out on something? *Are drugs really that bad for me?* he wondered. *They seem like candy here. It is like that roller coaster I was always too scared to ride . . . but when I did ride it, it was the best. Everyone seems like a family here; and I feel left out. If drugs are so wrong, why does everyone seem so happy? And why do I feel so stupid for not taking them?*

Ethan was frustrated. He had always thought that taking drugs was really dumb, but now everything seemed different. He had pictured druggies to be dressed in black leather, to have ugly faces, and to carry beepers. He was disillusioned when the beautiful brunette with deep blue eyes came up to him and offered him acid like it was a lollipop

Ethan ended up saying, "God, right now I do not understand why drugs are so wrong. I really want to take them. I know you've got to be right, so I won't do it. But please show me why they are wrong because I am angry that I can't do what I want to do!"

Ethan went home miserable. He felt separated from his friends who were all taking drugs that "opened their eyes up to the world." But he also felt a deepening inside him because he hadn't done what seemed fine to him at the time. He had decided, reluctantly, to let go of his will and his urging desires and to follow God's will. As bad as he felt, he was eventually glad about his decision.

Over a period of time God answered Ethan's prayer and showed him what drugs—even the innocent-looking ones—can do. He saw his friends flaking out on everything and everyone. They skipped school a lot more often. They couldn't find jobs, or if they found one they lost it quickly. They didn't care much about their friends or any of their activities. They didn't even care much about themselves, although they were deceived into thinking that they did. At first they kept looking forward to the next weekend when they could do their stuff, but then they started doing drugs on weekdays, and some moved on to bigger doses. They lost weight, and they always looked "burned." They had to beg or steal money to buy their drugs.

Ethan's friends thought they were so smart by living to please themselves. But Ethan could see that they were trapped, slaves to their chemical dependence. They weren't in control at all; they were being controlled by the drugs.

Ethan saw all this, and he understood what it meant to be free in Christ. God was not controlling Ethan like these drugs were controlling his friends' lives. Ethan had made the choice to break away from those tempting situations and friends and to accept Christ's forgiveness. What he got was freedom. God was still giving him the freedom to choose to follow Him or to become a slave to sin. He couldn't believe how close he had come to choosing to be a slave.

P. S.: If you have an addiction, please get help! I did not go to drug books to get this example. It is a true story that happened to a friend of mine in California.

For sin shall not have dominion over you, for you are not under law but under grace.

Romans 6:14

20

Is It All a Lie?

*I*f you have never read C. S. Lewis's *Chronicles of Narnia*, then stop reading this book right now and go get one of the books in that series! I cannot express how much those seven books have shaped my life. They have brought God alive to me in a way I never could have imagined. I can read them over and over again, enjoying them more and learning more from them. In fact, remembering an episode from the first book, *The Lion, the Witch, and the Wardrobe*, made me think about something I want to share with you.

It all begins with Lucy, the youngest of a group of children who are visiting a big, old house in northern England. Lucy finds an old wardrobe, which she enters. As she proceeds, she steps into the magical Land of Narnia, where she stays for hours. Then she comes back to the real world and runs to tell her brothers and sister of her experience. The problem is that according to "earth time," Lucy has only been gone a couple of minutes. Lucy's brothers and sister don't think she would lie to them, but how can they believe that she was in Narnia for hours when they just saw her a few minutes before?

Finally the wise old man who owns the house helps Lucy's brother and sister understand the truth. He logically points out that if Lucy were lying or making up a story, then she probably would have waited an hour or two to come out and tell them, making her story more believable. The fact that Lucy did come back only a couple of minutes after she had left makes her story *more* believable, not less.

I think the same logic applies to the story of Jesus. Not many people dispute that Jesus actually lived because He's in history books. But a lot of people question whether He was the Son of God who rose from the dead. They think the biblical account is just a myth or a lie. But if Jesus' story were really a lie, don't you think it would have been a lot different?

I mean, do you think that if someone decided to make up a story about how the Son of God, the Creator of the heavens and the earth, came to earth, do you think that person would say He was born in a manger? Would any creative storyteller have presented a king—the King of kings—walking everywhere on His own feet or swaying on a donkey instead of riding in a chariot or being carried by a bunch of servants? What good liar would have tried to tell us that the Son of God spent most of his time with people like tax collectors and fishermen instead of with the important people in government and society?

And what about miracles? If you had any imagination at all, would you make up something about a carpenter who turned water into wine? Not that Jesus' miracles weren't amazing, but think about it. This is the God who created all of the waterfalls, oceans, seas, rivers, and springs. He created all of the fruits, including the grapes to make wine. If someone were making up a story about the Son of God, then he would probably have Him leap over mountains or wipe out a whole army with a word. Jesus obviously could do all of those things; instead, He spent His time turning water into wine and feeding crowds with bread and fish and healing ordinary sick people and holding children in His lap.

If someone were just lying about the whole "Jesus thing," surely he would have come up with a better story! Jesus would not have died a common criminal's death in His early thirties. And

even if He had, His resurrection would have made a much bigger impact at the time. He wouldn't have shown His resurrected self to only a few hundred people. (If I were writing the story, I'd have Him go back to Pontius Pilate and say, "I'm back!")

If you are going to tell a lie, you are usually going to make it a good one. It would be absolutely ridiculous for a person to risk lying just to say that Jesus, the Son of God, was born in a manger, died as a criminal, and was raised up, completely surprising the people who had lived with Him the past two to three years.

I'm sure you can think about all of this for yourself; I wanted to express a little of what I was thinking. A lie by its very nature is often far more believable than what really happened. That's why it is often easier to tell a lie—and believe a lie—than the truth.

> **You are of your father the devil, and the desires of your father you want to do. He . . . does not stand in the truth, because there is no truth in him. When he speaks a lie, he speaks from his own resources, for he is a liar and the father of it. But because I tell the truth, you do not believe Me.**
>
> **John 8:44–45**

21

Does God Love Gay People?

he other night, a bunch of us were sitting in a restaurant, and our waiter seemed obviously gay. Well, several of the people I was with started rolling their eyes and mimicking the waiter behind his back. And that made me think. *How am I, as a Christian straight person, supposed to act toward someone who is homosexual?*

It's something we all have to think about. With the movement toward gay rights, even in the church, it's not something we can ignore. Homosexuality may even be a very personal issue for you right now. Maybe you have a friend who is gay, or even a parent. (It happens!) Or maybe you've struggled with homosexual feelings yourself.

Well, I don't have all the answers, but this is what makes sense to me. First of all, I think straight people need to learn to have compassion for and try to understand all people, including those who prefer people of their own sex. And that's because it's easy for a person's thinking to get distorted, often through no fault of their own.

I know many women—and some men—who have struggled with eating disorders. And I know that a person with anorexia starves herself because she really thinks her body is fat. Well, something's obviously wrong with the thinking of a woman who is five feet seven, weighs eighty-four pounds, and truly thinks she's fat.

I am not saying that homosexuals are mental or, for that matter, that anorexics are. I just know that a person's view of reality can get distorted. And if we have compassion for an anorexic with her misconceptions, we need to have compassion for homosexuals as well. (If you have homosexual feelings, that applies to you, too. The first thing you need to do is have compassion for yourself! God does.)

Now, I've always wondered why homosexuals prefer people of their own gender in the first place. My father is a psychiatrist, so I asked him for his professional opinion. I learned that you cannot point to just one reason a person becomes homosexual. There are many possible reasons, just as there are many reasons a person may become anorexic. However, most of the homosexual men my father has counseled seem to share some common factors. Often these men, as children, were not close to their fathers when they were little, especially when they were between the ages of three to six. They had no one to imitate or to show them what a male should be like, so they imitated what they saw in their moms. They also yearned for love and connection with their fathers because they never had it, and eventually, somehow, things got turned around.

Again, this isn't always the case. But I can certainly see how something like that would happen, and it would certainly not be the child's fault. I don't believe anybody has a right to condemn another person for a set of circumstances he or she has no control over, and that includes having feelings for and being tempted to have a sexual relationship with someone of the same gender.

But—and this is important—being tempted is *not* the same thing as giving in to temptation. And God has given us a whole set of temptations we are not to give in to. For instance, He has told us that we are not supposed to have sex outside of marriage. If you're protesting, "But that's not the same thing," stop a minute and think. To homosexuals, the idea of having sex with someone of the same gender seems natural, almost like having sex outside of marriage seems natural to many heterosexuals in the world today. But in either case, God has told us not to do it.

Remember, it's easy for us humans to get our thinking and our feelings distorted, but that doesn't change what is right or what is good for us. What if I grew up in the jungle and found myself tempted to have a relationship with an animal? Would that mean it was right? No, because I was not made by God to be with an animal. And the Bible makes it very clear that men are not made to be with men and women are not made to be with women. God made man and woman for each other, and He made sex for men and women in a marriage relationship. For our own good He tells us to live within those guidelines.

What does all this mean practically? If you have temptations for someone of your own sex, do not feel ashamed and full of guilt for having those temptations. You've probably developed them because of someone else's sins. On the other hand, just because you *feel* like having sex with someone does not mean that you should go off and do it! If you have feelings for someone of your own sex, you really should go to a Christian counselor who can help you. (I say a Christian counselor because many non-Christian counselors will advise you to be yourself and to go ahead and act on your feelings. It would be wrong to act on that advice.) And please do not think that your Heavenly Father is going to ignore you as perhaps your father or mother has ignored you.

If you're straight, you need to have compassion for gay people. Encourage them to go to a counselor—not because they are crazy, but because, like the anorexic, they have a distorted picture of what the truth is. Most of all, don't assume that just because they're gay you have the right to make fun of them or mistreat them in any way. God's pretty clear about that kind of temptation, too!

God calls homosexual acts sin in both the Old and New Testaments, but God loves those who have homosexual temptations just as much as He loves those of us who have heterosexual temptations. He also offers forgiveness and new life to all of us who are tempted to sin in any way.

> **Do not be deceived. Neither fornicators, nor idolaters, nor adulterers, *nor homosexuals* . . . nor thieves, nor covetous, nor drunkards, nor revilers, nor extortioners will inherit the kingdom of God. *And such were some of you.* But you were washed, but you were sanctified, but you were justified in the name of the Lord Jesus and by the Spirit of our God.**
>
> **1 Corinthians 6:9–11**

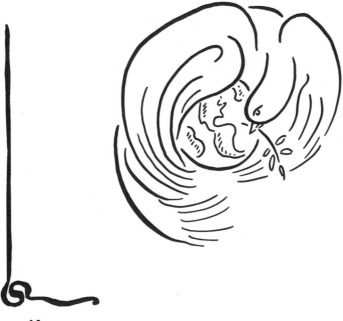

22

What's On Tonight?

ast night I truly considered throwing my TV set in the dumpster! I flipped it on for a few minutes so that I could relax. A guy was blowing a woman away with a gun. So I changed channels. There is a room full of teenagers drinking and making out. Click. The Three Stooges poking each other in the eye. Click. Two women selling a combination vegetable slicer and juicer (with free steak knives!) Click. It's off.

I know it's not always like that. I have found lots of good stuff on TV. I certainly am not saying you should only watch reruns of "Little House on the Prairie." What you watch is your decision, not mine. I just think it's a good idea to consider what we are watching and why we might want to avoid some of it. (I think now is a good time to remind you that I am only nineteen, and I do not have an adult on my back telling me to write this!)

Let's start with a sitcom I saw recently. The dad on the show was leering lustfully at a young woman who was visiting. "So what?" you may ask. Well, if you are a female you can probably relate to being looked at like a piece of meat. It is *not* cool! It is usually the same guys who look at you like a piece of meat who would also use you or take advantage of you.

Think about this for a second. When you start looking at a person lustfully, you are dehumanizing him or her. You are looking at him or her as you would look at a piece of chocolate cake . . . as an object to satisfy your appetite, to use for your pleasure. Thanks, but I think I will pass on being somebody else's piece of meat or chocolate cake! And I don't think I want to watch a person treating somebody else that way on TV.

I'm not saying we should retreat to a dark, secluded room to protect our holy minds. I think that would do more harm than if we went to a decent movie with one questionable scene. But we do need to be alert to the lies and the wrong and make sure we don't file them in our minds as the truth.

And I think there are times when we should decide *not* to see something by turning the TV off. Things we see tend to stick with us, whether we want them to or not. I will tell you now that I really regret some of the things that I have seen; it is difficult to get the images out of my mind. And things we see and hear over and over usually influence our attitudes and behavior.

If I am around someone who is cursing all the time, then those words start formulating themselves in my mind. If I'm around people who yell at each other or cheat, it starts feeling more "right" to yell or cheat. And I think that the more we see people on the screen having casual sex—or even arranging casual murders—the more likely we are to believe incorrectly that those things are acceptable or inevitable.

Sometimes I think we even *want* to believe some of the lies! We want to hear that cheating on your boyfriend is okay. We want to see that everybody cheats on their exams. We want to see that everybody drinks under age or talks bad about their friends, so that we can justify these things in our minds.

There's no law that says you have to watch TV, even when the shows are okay. Believe it or not, there are lots more fun and better things to do—like skateboarding, riding a bike, taking a walk with friends, or lying on the grass and enjoying the breeze! Think about what life was like before TV was even invented.

I am not saying that I never watch TV and you should never watch it either. I think that is a little extreme! TV can be fun. But is it replacing the time you spend with other people? Is it helping you avoid life altogether or getting you used to ideas and actions that are clearly wrong?

I don't think we should be paranoid, just aware of what is on and how much time we actually spend watching it.

Stay away from a foolish man,
for you will not find knowledge on his lips.
The wisdom of the prudent is to give thought to their ways,
but the folly of fools is deception.
Proverbs 14:7–8 (NIV)

Finally, brothers, whatever is true, whatever is noble,
whatever is right, whatever is pure, whatever is lovely,
whatever is admirable—if anything is excellent or
praiseworthy—think about such things.
Philippians 4:8 (NIV)

23

Look at Me!

Sean is a really good-looking guy who always dresses nicely. He always gets attention because many women find him attractive. And after about seventeen or eighteen years of this kind of approval, Sean is accustomed to using his looks to his advantage.

When Sean likes someone, he knows just what to do. First, he goes out and buys a new shirt to wear with his black jeans. He works hard to make his hair look perfect. Then he goes out to where the girls are, knowing that if he acts cool and gives her his smile, she'll jump at the chance to go out with him. How can she help herself once she sees how good-looking he is?

But this time it doesn't happen. Maybe the girl Sean likes wants to play hard to get. Maybe she thinks he's conceited. Or maybe she doesn't think that a guy as good-looking as Sean could like her. Maybe she's been wondering what he's really like, but is waiting for him to come over and talk to her.

And Sean doesn't have a clue. He keeps trying to impress her by looking good. He acts interested in other girls who he knows will react immediately to his silent calling. Once he has about five girls hanging around him, maybe he'll work up the courage to approach the girl he really likes. But she still doesn't seem interested in him, so he acts more cocky and walks away. Inside, however, Sean is depressed. His looks have always worked for him. What went wrong?

Well, we go across the room to where Tricia is sitting, and we see what went wrong. When Tricia came in she immediately saw Sean and noticed how good-looking he was, but she turned to her friends and started thinking. Tricia felt like she could relate to Sean; she could see right through the little games he was playing because she had played the same ones!

Tricia is an attractive seventeen-year-old, and she used to be obsessed with the way she looked. She was always on a diet, and was always working out. She shopped for the right makeup and the most flattering clothes. It would take her almost an hour just to do her hair the way she wanted it. And she always got plenty of attention for the way she looked!

But Tricia got tired of people coming up to her because they wanted her to look good next to them. She also got tired of people being interested only in what she looked like and not valuing who she was inside.

Tricia still cares about her appearance, and sometimes she has to struggle to keep a balanced attitude. But she is not obsessed about it anymore; she realizes that she needs and wants to get to know people for who they are. Tricia probably would talk with Sean if he approached her and let her see what is behind the mask. But she's not interested in playing the same old game she used to play.

A big part of Sean's and Tricia's problem is the habit of basing self-worth on how a person looks rather than on who that person is . . . or better yet, who he or she is in Christ. The Bible is clear that God doesn't value us by how we look. Although God does not rely upon outward appearance, we human beings certainly do, at least part of the time. I know that I go through stages when I just go crazy because I don't think I look good.

When I act like Sean and start to get obsessed with my looks, I am *always* let down, one way or another. I can't win. If people don't think I'm beautiful—and even the most successful supermodel is considered unattractive by some people—

then I feel rejected. If people are attracted to me because of my looks, I wonder whether they would like me for the person inside. Besides, what happens if I'm in an accident or something and become scarred or disfigured? What happens when I start getting older?

So how can I get a better perspective on myself and how I look? The change starts inside, when I start thinking like God intended me to think. When I start seeing myself for what I am, created in God's image, then sometimes (but not always) others will also see me that way.

I think God did intend for us to enjoy and admire beauty—and to do the best we can with what we have—but a face and body can only go so far. When you start getting to know other people and seeing *beyond* their looks, that is what is really beautiful!

Who cares about the beautiful wrapping paper and ribbons around a present? Some of the best presents I've seen were wrapped in newspaper and given by a loving friend!

If you feel frustrated because you don't feel like you are pretty enough or handsome enough, I hope you can begin to realize that when you get older most people value *who* you are more. Just think, that means you have a head start in developing meaningful relationships.

Man looks at the outward appearance, but the LORD looks at the heart.

1 Samuel 16:7

24

I Was Pressured into It

o one needs to use the excuse, "I was pressured into it." Yes, it happens. And yes, I have felt pressure to do something wrong. Sometimes I have done it, and sometimes I have not. But it was my choice every time. No one, unless they use force, can make you do anything.

If you are a Christian, you have the ability not to do something. God has given you the power in Christ to overcome sin. I'm not saying you will be wholly without sin, because 1 John 1:8 says you'd be lying if you said that. But you are not a slave to sin anymore, so you never have to do what's wrong.

God has given us the power to resist pressure. He convicts us with the Holy Spirit and directs us with His word.

What more do we want Him to do . . . make all sinful things disappear? That might be a lot easier, but calling on God builds a lot more character.

And you may be saying, "Character, what is that? And who really cares? I'd rather have another drink than character."

Well, I can't define character completely. But I can tell you that when I refuse something because I know it is wrong, and when I trust God's judgment instead of my own, I am being worked on by God. It's a cool thing!

Let's use an example here. Let's imagine that I want to share myself with the man I love . . . in other words, have premarital sex. And let's imagine that I want to so badly that I'm in tears. Well, when I stay away from situations that are leading me that way, I am doing God's will and not the will of my flesh. God made sex. And sex is beautiful at the right time, which is when you have a lifetime commitment to one another. Saying no to what my flesh wants and yes to what God wants makes me gradually become more like Christ, which is the way God intended me to be from the beginning! Therefore, when I say no to my burning passions and yes to Christ in me, I might feel pain in the process but I'll be happier in the long run.

Once again, it's your choice. You're going to feel the pressure . . . I do. But remember, you don't have to give in.

> **No temptation has overtaken you except such as is common to man; but God is faithful, who will not allow you to be tempted beyond what you are able, but with the temptation will also make the way of escape, that you may be able to bear it.**
> **1 Corinthians 10:13**

25

It's Okay, You Are Just Curious

ible study was tonight, and Alicia could not wait to get there. She had missed last week, so she was really behind on what was going on in everybody's life. She wanted to find out who was cheating on her boyfriend . . . who had been caught drinking . . . who wasn't speaking to whom . . . and who had the worst family problems. Alicia loved going to this Bible study because of prayer time. That was when all the "best stuff" was shared. Any time Alicia felt a little guilty about hearing or telling something about somebody else, she quickly reminded herself that she had to know these things in order to pray specifically for these people's needs. She easily justified her behavior because she could call her gossip "prayer and share time."

It seems to me that the world we live in right now is breaking—and making all kinds of justifications for breaking—all of the morals and ethics that have been here from the beginning.

Take the 1992 Los Angeles riot for example. (This is a big thing for me because I was living in the L.A. area at the time.) In normal conditions, almost everybody would agree that it is wrong to steal from a store. Well, when *everyone* was stealing, and when it was all blamed on the verdict (the riots were sparked when three white policemen accused of beating a black man were acquitted), people of all races and nationalities seemed to have no problem taking whatever they wanted.

Well, believe it or not it works this way on many, many other issues. In the past, according to most moral codes (not just the Judeo-Christian one), having sex with lots of people either before marriage or outside of marriage was just plain wrong. Sure, people did it, but at least they were aware it wasn't the moral thing to do. But now people don't even talk about the morality of premarital sex, but about "safe sex"—as if any sex outside of marriage is safe, either physically or emotionally. Some say, "I would only do it if I really loved the person," yet they don't love the other person enough to commit to a lifetime together. And people don't commit adultery; they have affairs or just a fling. And as long as everyone is responsible and adult, nobody seems to think anything about it.

What is the deal here? Are we going to be that naïve to believe that something is okay just because more people are doing it or because something else bad has happened or because we have simply decided to call our actions by another name?

The thing to do when we go against God's laws is to wake up, repent, ask for and receive forgiveness, and not try to justify ourselves or blame others for our choices. We need to reach out for strength and encouragement from others who value the truth. It has been here from the beginning. The truth that God created and that Christianity supports is a way to live (through Christ) and to overcome the denial that the world is accepting.

The Bible says that Satan is the prince of this world who disguises himself as an angel of light. He is not going to use the word *promiscuous,* but *curious.* He'll urge us to turn cheating on a test into a form of cooperative learning, to see lying as merely exaggeration or a half-truth. (Why don't we call it a half-lie?) And he loves it when we pour down alcohol or drugs or even junk food, all the while telling ourselves, *I don't have a problem.*

It's so frustrating to me that Christians can be so blind and deceived! I am not saying I am beyond it either. For instance, it is easy for me to believe the lie that I am worthless and have no value here on earth. If that were true, then God either would not have created me or would have taken me out of here a lot sooner!

It's so easy for us to be blinded to the reality of evil in our world. That's why we need to encourage each other and challenge each other as brothers and sisters. Do not let me or anyone else tell you what the absolute truth is; read it for yourself in the Word of God! Pastors, teachers, artists, and others can help you understand, but always check what they say—and most definitely what the world says—against the Bible.

Do not be deceived. God knows you, and He needs you to stand up for the truth in a world where so many blind people are leading all the other deceived people straight into the pit of pain.

We need to stop making excuses for, or changing the names of, the sins that we keep repeating. We need to confess them for what they are, and receive the forgiveness found only in Christ.

> **Some things . . . are hard to understand, which ignorant and unstable people distort, as they do the other Scriptures, to their own destruction. Therefore, dear friends, since you already know this, be on your guard so that you may not be carried away by the error of lawless men and fall from your secure position. But grow in the grace and knowledge of our Lord and Savior Jesus Christ.**
>
> **2 Peter 3:16–18 (NIV)**

26

Winning God's Approval

$\mathcal{N}$icole is a girl who tries hard and usually succeeds at everything she does. She gets mostly A's in school and is good at gymnastics, track, and cheerleading. She's a leader in her youth group at church and her local branch of Young Life.

Everybody is always praising Nicole for how well she is doing in classes, for how much she is improving her running times, for how spectacular the cheerleading squad's last cheer was at half time, and even for how nice a person she is. And Nicole loves it. In fact, she always tries to be extra polite and helpful to people so they will enjoy being around her and give her even more praise. She also goes out of her way to avoid confronting others. She would much rather inconvenience herself than to have somebody be mad at her.

And it's not long before Nicole is looking at God the way she looks at everyone else. If she doesn't live her life just right, she thinks, maybe God will be disappointed in her. Maybe He'll love her less, or else knock her down on his list of people he likes a lot.

So Nicole starts trying harder to earn God's praise. She gets up half an hour early every morning to have her quiet time, has an hour-long quiet time after school, and memorizes Scripture right before bed. She goes to a Bible study on Tuesdays, a

church group on Wednesdays, Young Life on Thursdays, and church on Sundays.

Nicole soon stops doing some of the things she likes. She drives exactly the speed limit. She gives up dancing and listening to secular music. She stops going to parties with her friends (even though she didn't drink or anything before). She refuses to see even PG rated movies, and she even limits her TV time to one hour a week.

Dating, well, that could be trouble so Nicole backs off. She stops eating desserts . . . that might be leaning toward gluttony. She even stops drinking sodas (diet or otherwise) because someone tells her that carbonation might be bad for her health, and her body is supposed to be a temple of God.

Before long, Nicole is having trouble understanding why her other Christian friends are so "sinful." They drink Coke for lunch and eat a huge chocolate chip cookie! They listen to and sing Amy Grant's secular songs. She's not trying to judge them— and she would never confront them! But she still begins to look down on her friends and to feel uncomfortable around them. (They're getting pretty uncomfortable around her, too.)

One night Nicole goes to her regular Young Life meeting, and Kathy, one of her leaders, pulls her aside. Kathy does not say much, except that some of Nicole's friends have talked to her because they are feeling hurt by Nicole. Nicole cannot see how she's hurt her friends, but Kathy gives her a list of verses to look up. Nicole eagerly takes them, hoping they'll show her how to be a better Christian. She goes home that night and begins looking up the verses one by one and writing them down as she finds them.

The first two verses were Romans 14:4 and 14:10. "Who are you to judge another's servant? . . . Why do you judge your brother? Or why do you show contempt for your brother? For we shall all stand before the judgment seat of Christ."

The third verse was Matthew 7:4. "Or how can you say to

your brother, 'Let me remove the speck from your eye'; and look, a plank is in your own eye?"

By now, Nicole has started to cry. She has been so busy looking at outward acts—hers and everyone else's—that she has forgotten that God cares most about the attitude of our hearts. These words that Jesus said to the Pharisees were offensive to them, and they are hard for Nicole to swallow, too. She starts to wonder how God could still love her after she has been so blind and after she has hurt her friends, who are really struggling to serve God.

Nicole's problem is that she has been basing her idea of who she is in God's sight on what she does, which is *never* going to be good enough for God. He is perfect and demands perfection, which none of us can measure up to. That's why Christ died for us . . . to take the burden of perfection upon Himself, and to free us from the burden of always having to measure up.

Fortunately, Nicole's slip-up is a new beginning for her. With the help of Kathy and some good friends, Nicole goes through a process of understanding and feeling God's love and forgiveness. She begins to realize that God cares more about why she does things, her inner motives, than He does about her specific actions. God will not love her more or less if she wears jeans to church or even skips church sometimes. His love is constant and unconditional, unlike that of her human pastors, parents, friends, and teachers.

Nicole still messes up from time to time. She violates God's principles and does things she knows are not right. But her world does not cave in when that happens because she knows God will not leave her. (She's learning to stand up to other people, too.) Nicole has actually learned to love Jesus more for the free forgiveness He has given her. His unconditional acceptance makes her want to do the right things instead of feeling like she has to do them to win God's approval!

Are you so foolish? After beginning with the Spirit, are you now trying to attain your goal by human effort? . . . Now that faith has come, we are no longer under the supervision of the law.

Galatians 3:3, 25 (NIV)

27

Your
Perfect Parent

*L*ibby's father was hardly ever around when she was growing up. He was a missionary. He really loved God and was devoted to sharing his faith with others. But most of the time he was so busy sharing the good news that he couldn't take time off to spend with his family. Libby knew that her father worked hard doing God's work. Everybody talked about what a godly man he was. So why did she feel so hurt and neglected?

By the time she was fourteen or fifteen, Libby had started to think that maybe God was like her father. Surely He had more important things to do than to pay attention to her needs and her hurts and her prayers. Surely He couldn't take time to listen to her and care for her! So why bother God in the first place? Libby just got used to handling her life without Him.

Have you ever thought about what your parents' shortcomings may be doing to your idea of God? Think about it. The Bible says that God is our father (and mother, too, in a lot of ways). It compares His love for us to a parent's love. And that's great if I have loving, mature parents who make all the right decisions and provide the right mix of tenderness and discipline.

But what if I grew up with my father beating on me whenever I got in his way? I would probably grow up trying to be a perfect Christian all the time so that I could stay out of God's way. (Or maybe I would avoid having anything to do with Him.)

Or what if I grew up with a smothering mom who would run to comfort me every time I cried or scrunched up my face? I would probably cry to God a lot and expect Him to come running to take care of every little hurt.

What if both of my parents ignored me all the time, no matter what I did? I guess I would probably do whatever I wanted because I would assume God didn't have time for me either.

Now, most of our parents do the best job they can loving us. We need to understand that their love is not perfect, but God's love is. Would it not be weird if our parents took a whole day out . . . or even just an hour . . . and listened attentively to every word we said? Well, God hears *every* word we say twenty-four hours a day. Psalm 139:4 says that even before a word is on my tongue God knows it completely. God not only knows what we are going to say, but He cares deeply about our emotions, needs, desires, feelings, hurts . . . everything!

God loves us even if our parents abandon us. He loves us when our parents give us what we want when they should be disciplining us. God loves us when we fail our exams, don't clean our rooms, or whatever. God's love is *always*. It doesn't stop and start again like other people's love does, even parents' love.

It is so hard for me to understand this sometimes because I can feel so distant from God, like He is leaving me to deal with life on my own. But He says in His Word that He will never leave me nor forsake me, even when I feel like no one cares. I'm still trying to understand why I have such a hard time feeling His love sometimes, but I do know He's right here beside me, and He's beside you, too!

It's hard sometimes, especially when your parents are exasperating, but try not to forget or lose sight of how much God truly loves you. Try to think as a Christian. And study the Word of God, which will show you the truth and keep reminding you about God's love for you. It never ends and it never decreases. He's the perfect parent you never had.

If you then, being evil, know how to give good gifts to your children, how much more will your Father who is in heaven give good things to those who ask Him!

Matthew 7:11

28

Pray
for Peace

*E*lizabeth had been at camp for a month. She was so excited to see her friends and parents after the long break. She ran up to her house after the long bus ride home and she crashed open the door. "Mom . . . Dad . . . I'm home!"

It was good to see all the familiar things in the house, but something felt wrong. She got silent all of a sudden and looked in the living room. One of the couches was missing. She ran up the stairs to her parents' room and noticed that her father's closet was empty. What was going on?

"Elizabeth!" she heard her mom's voice from below, then her mom's footsteps climbing the stairs. Elizabeth just stood there. "Mom, what's going on?" Her mom tried to smile and give Elizabeth a hug, but Elizabeth wouldn't respond. "Mom, where is Dad? What's going on?"

Then Elizabeth's mother sat down on the bed with her and began to cry. She confessed that she and Elizabeth's dad had been having a lot of problems, and they had decided the best time to go through a separation was while the kids were away at camp.

Elizabeth could not believe it; she didn't want to believe it. She had had no idea that things were so bad between her parents. There had been arguments, but she had never thought they were serious. Now her mom was mumbling something about spending Christmas with Dad . . . every other weekend . . . moving to a smaller house. . . .

Elizabeth ran to her room and fell on her bed, crying. She started yelling in her pillow, "God, what is going on? Why is this happening to me? Was it my fault? Did I do something wrong? I am so afraid, God. Are You still here? Are You going to leave too? What am I supposed to do?"

She had felt so full of peace before she walked into the house. Now she just wanted to erase all the disorder that had just fallen into her life.

When it seems like our world is falling apart, how can we be at peace?

Are we supposed to act like nothing bothers us? Does being at peace mean we don't respond at all to our surroundings or the things that happen to us?

I think it means having a sense that no matter what happens to you, you will be okay.

You can usually tell when people have inner peace. Not that they smile when their car blows up in front of them or when their boyfriend or girlfriend wants to break up. No, these people hurt and cry and get angry when bad things happen. But they are not in complete despair because they know that Christ is in them. At a deep level, they are confident that His love and grace are enough for them, and that this life is short compared to eternity with God. You can tell somehow that these people know God is in control.

Peace does not necessarily mean always feeling happy or serene. I don't think God intends for us to laugh and say "Yippee!" when bad things are happening. (That would be lying or fooling ourselves, and God is a God of truth.) But we can still have an inner peace, knowing that everything will work out in the end.

Sometimes that sense of peace is hard to come by—and

I've really struggled with it recently. But I still believe it's something we can pray for and grow into.

What things are bothering you right now? Your parents divorcing? Brother or sister into drugs? Entering a new school? A friend who's been killed in a car accident? You would be a machine if you smiled about any of that! But you can still pray for peace inside, and somehow God will answer that prayer. We know God allows evil people to do evil things, but He also promises to see us through the evil we experience in this world.

If you look at the difference between Christ's apostles and Christ, you will clearly see the difference His peace can make. They would get anxious and caught up in dealing with how they were going to feed those five thousand people and how they were going to get to the other side of the Sea of Galilee in such a terrible storm. But Jesus wasn't that way; He trusted that God would provide. He was sleeping in the boat during the storm, and the disciples had to wake Him.

Jesus calmed the storm with a word and everything became silent. I think the water was just reflecting the perfect peace that was inside of Jesus.

Now, let's think here. God says that He wants me to have peace in my heart and life. With one word, God the Son calmed the storm. I'm sure it would not be a problem for God to teach me how to have inner peace if I ask Him.

Peace I leave with you, My peace I give to you; not as the world gives do I give to you. Let not your heart be troubled, neither let it be afraid.

John 14:27

29

All by Myself

*I*t was a long, quiet weekend. A lot of my friends were out of town. My parents didn't call. It was just me in my apartment, by myself, the whole weekend. It was so much fun! Why do so many people think that solitude is bad?

Yes, I think that people need each other to talk to, to spend time with, and to love. We learn so much from spending time with others. But what's wrong with spending time alone, too?

Didn't Jesus spend forty days in the wilderness by Himself preparing for His ministry? Didn't Jesus wake up early in the morning before the sun was rising to go pray alone? Doesn't the Bible say that Jesus would go off without the disciples to spend the whole night praying on a mountain?

I don't know if you have ever gotten the opportunity to sit alone on the top of a mountain before. I did when I was in Israel. And it seems to me that even an atheist would have to be praying and thanking God for such an experience. It was so beautiful!

I do my best thinking when I am alone and when I am not doing my homework, not on the phone, not listening to the radio or watching TV, not reading a novel, and not obsessing about something in my head to avoid facing myself. (Even if no one's around, I'm not truly alone if I'm doing something to avoid facing myself or God.)

I do a lot of growing when I'm all by myself in a quiet place. I can struggle with my doubts and fears, pray about them, and

listen for God's answers. I can examine my beliefs about God the Father and Christ the Son, or read and reread the Scriptures and try to figure out what they are saying and how I can interpret and use them in my life. Being with other people also helps me grow, but I've found that I need those times alone to more fully understand God and deal with reality.

If I wanted to, I could be a Christian most of my life and hardly ever be alone. I mean, there are church activities to go to and meetings to attend every night of the week in some places! But unless people take time out to be alone, to think and reflect about what they are hearing and reading, they are robbing themselves of an opportunity for healing and growth.

My friend, Gina, who spends thirty minutes a week of silence and solitude just thinking about and talking to God, is probably getting more quality time than someone else who goes to a million classes and services and Bible studies each week. There is so much we can learn in silence!

My soul, wait silently for God alone,
For my expectation is from Him.

Psalm 62:5

30

Is Anyone There for Me?

C had sat on his bed, staring at the phone in his room. His friends had called and left him messages all week, but he just had not gotten around to calling them back. He began to think about what was going on in his life with work, school, church, and family. How could he be involved in all that stuff and still feel so alone and cut off from people? He felt there was no one in his life he could open up to, no one who cared what was going on in his mind.

His family tended to make him feel like he was supposed to be totally self-sufficient, like he was not allowed to have any needs. As for his friends, well, he would spend time with them going to movies, to church, or to some other activity, but he never talked with them about anything deep. He had tried it with a few of his friends, and it seemed like every time he opened up with someone, they would reject him or put him down or not take him seriously.

Chad wanted to reach out to other people and be honest with them and find out what they were all about. He wanted to share his thoughts, dreams, fears, and desires. But he couldn't bring himself to trust another person that much.

He had talked to God, telling him how lonely he felt. He had expected God to fix the problem and take away his loneliness, but it had not happened. So he had surrounded himself with

work and church activities to cover up the lonely feelings. But whenever he was alone they always resurfaced.

"God, what do I do?" he wrote in his journal. "I know that You want us to love others and to reach out, but I guess I am really hurt and scared. I am not ready to let someone else see the inside of me and step on it again. I would rather be alone than let that happen again. Isn't there a way for You to take away these lonely feelings and keep me protected? God, is there anyone out there I can trust, who won't betray me or talk bad about me when my back is turned? God, what am I supposed to do? I feel like I am inside of this cage that I have the keys to, but I'm too scared to set myself free."

I really know how Chad feels. I know what it feels like to be lonely, to isolate myself, to want to share so much with a another person, but instead I keep it locked inside because people have undervalued me and stepped on me before.

Life can be awful sometimes. People hurt you. People put you down. People don't take you seriously. (Many times they do this because someone else has hurt them, but that doesn't make their rejection any easier to live with.)

The problem is that when you begin to care for a person on a deep level, you are opening up to him or her. I wish so much that we could push a button on the other person that would make him or her care for us the same way, but that is not the way it works. With relationships there has to be a free choice. The other person can choose to care about us or not.

When another person chooses to take advantage of the love or friendship we have offered, it really hurts. But we cannot control how other people make their choices. God does not control our choices, but allows us to choose to follow Him and return His love or we can abuse it and throw it back in His face.

How do you think Jesus felt when He loved us so much that He died for us and the people that had been following Him were now yelling, "Crucify Him! Crucify Him!"? They were jeering at Him as He was hanging on the cross, and He still prayed, "Father, forgive them, for they do not know what they do" (Luke 23:34). They spat on His love, yet He continued to offer it.

God wants us to love each other, not to exploit one another, take advantage of one another, or hurt each other. He made us so He could have a relationship with us and we could have relationships with others. But how can we do that when there is so much hurt in the world? How can we open up when we know we might be rejected or ignored?

Well, God warns us, "Do not give what is holy to the dogs; nor cast your pearls before swine, lest they trample them under their feet, and turn and tear you in pieces" (Matthew 7:6). I think that God is telling us to be cautious about choosing whom we open up to. But running from everyone is not the answer either.

Real friends are like a glimpse of heaven. They are people you can be honest with, people who will love you and show you grace even though they know the bad things about you, and people who can confront you and be real with you. Don't throw that away because someone else in your life decided to reject your love. Real love can heal what wrong love has wounded.

Talk to God about the hurts you have. Look for people who show real love for God and for others. God will put people in your life who you can trust. It is so important for you to keep on trusting Him, keep on going to Him with your fears, and then to keep reaching out to other people. Reach out slowly if you have to. You can even be honest and tell your friends that it is hard for you to reach out. But don't let other people's sins gyp you out of loving and being loved by people who will show you real love.

Remember, though, that human love will never be perfect. My love is not perfect, and yours isn't either. But God's love is. We can trust Him. And in Him we can learn how to love others with a real love.

Blessed be the God and Father of our Lord Jesus Christ, the Father of mercies and God of all comfort, who comforts us in all our tribulation, that we may be able to comfort those who are in any trouble, with the comfort with which we ourselves are comforted by God.

2 Corinthians 1:3–4

34

It's <u>My</u> Boyfriend (<u>My</u> Car, <u>My</u> House)!

Who or what on this earth do you love the most? Is it your best friend? Your music? Your car?

Now, ask yourself, *If God asked me to give up that person, or that thing, or that activity, would I do it?*

It's easy to answer automatically, "Oh, sure." Think about what it would mean to give up something that means a lot to you.

If you're honest, it's a hard question, and answering it can be difficult. But I've found that asking that question helps me get perspective on where I am with God.

For example, I love to dance . . . in my apartment, outside, in my car, anywhere. I sometimes feel that if I couldn't dance, well, I don't know what I would do. But then it's like I hear God asking, "Would you give that up if I thought you needed to?"

Or let's say I've started liking a guy. I can be so sure that someone is right for me, and it can be so easy to grab on tightly and put all my energy into that relationship. But here comes that question again. Would I be willing to give him up for God's sake?

The point is, God wants to be first in our lives. He wants to be more important to us than any person we care about, any activity we love, any possession that makes us feel good. He wants us to remember where we got all those good things in the first place and who's going to be around when they're all gone.

I have a friend who is older than I am. She and her husband worked for years and years to buy a house, and they were so excited when they finally signed the papers and moved in. Things were looking great . . . until the house caught fire and burned down.

The point is, nothing on this earth lasts forever. Stereos get stolen. Cars get wrecked. Boyfriends and girlfriends leave, and friends move away. Pets die. People die. Everything we call "mine" is a temporary gift from God. And the tighter and tighter we try to hold on to our possessions and our relationships, the more it is going to hurt when we lose what really wasn't ours in the first place!

I'm not saying we shouldn't value our possessions and our relationships. I'm not saying we should let our rooms or houses stay trashed and always wear dirty clothes and not care about our friends. We need to be good keepers or stewards of whatever God has let us have. But we should also try to keep in perspective that our possessions, and even our relationships, are always God's to give or to take away.

That's easy to say, I know. And it's really, really difficult to let go of something we care about—the lost boyfriend, the burned house, the wrecked convertible, the tons of friends we left behind when we moved, our popular days before we went to a college where no one knows us. But in any of these situations, while God might not have directly caused the loss, He allowed it. And He can teach us in this process, if we're open to learning.

When Job lost everything, his wife told him to "curse God and die." Her attitude was that life without a big house, lots of clothes, lots of children, lots of friends, lots of cattle, gardens, and perfect health was not worth living. But Job wisely replied that both good and bad are in God's hands. He chose to keep on trusting God:

Shall we indeed accept good from God, and shall we not accept adversity? . . . For I know that my Redeemer lives,

And He shall stand at last on the earth; And after my skin is destroyed, this know, that in my flesh I shall see God.
Job 2:10; 19:25–26

We're wise to keep that attitude, too. If it's hard for you to think about what you would do if God took one of your favorite things away from you, try it for a day. If you like TV, try taking the TV away from yourself for the afternoon. Or put away your stereo, or your favorite outfit, or the phone. (I wouldn't recommend doing this with people; they might not understand.)

However you do it, try to get a feel for how tight your grasp is on things and people. And then thank God for what you have because whatever it is, it's a gift.

Do not lay up for yourselves treasures on earth, where moth and rust destroy and where thieves break in and steal; but lay up for yourselves treasures in heaven, where neither moth nor rust destroys and where thieves do not break in and steal. For where your treasure is, there your heart will be also.

Matthew 6:19–21

32

This Devotional Is <u>Not</u> About Drinking!

*I*t's a loud, crowded party. The music's blasting. People are laughing, talking, and having a good time. Everyone is standing around casually drinking beer. And there you are, clutching your Coke, feeling stupid. And you're thinking, *Hmm, why did I decide that I didn't want to drink?*

But this is *not* a devotional about whether or not you should drink! You'll have to make that decision for yourself. My point here is that it's easy to get confused about issues of right and wrong. What starts out to be so clear in your head can become clouded by your experiences.

And that is why we, as Christians, cannot become lazy in our walk with God. If we make our decisions without thinking them through, without understanding why they make sense, we're going to be easily deceived. At least I know that's true for me. I have to know why I am "depriving myself" of what seems like a good time and looks harmless.

So where do we go to figure out the whys? My starting place is God, but I do not blindly refuse things and use God as my excuse. God has reasons for what He commands us to do. He does not tell us something to make us mad. And I think we are being lazy sometimes not to think about those reasons.

The reasons behind God's commandments are not always spelled out in the Bible. I mean, just think about how long the

Bible would be if after every command God said, "Don't disobey your parents because (1) . . . (2) . . . (3) . . . , etc. But examining the facts will usually show us that the biblical directions about what we should do really make sense.

Let's go back to the drinking example. What are some of the reasons I might decide that drinking is not for me, at least not now? For one thing, although the Bible doesn't actually say that Christians shouldn't drink alcohol, it does warn us against drunkenness (Prov. 23:29-35, 1 Cor. 6:9-10, Gal. 5:19-21, Eph. 5:18, 1 Pet. 4:3). And although drinking a beer at a party doesn't necessarily make you drunk, it does make getting drunk a lot more likely. That's especially true if the people around you are getting drunk, which is the purpose of some parties!

That's one reason. You may choose not to drink at that party because you know there's a good chance that you may get drunk. And it's not hard to understand why the Bible warns against that. All you have to do is look at some of the statistics and stories about drunk driving and alcoholism and date rape and alcohol as a depressant.

But here's another issue. The Bible directs Christians to obey all governing authorities, and it's against the law in the United States for people under age twenty-one to drink alcohol. It's not hard to understand the reasons behind that law either. People our age are still in the process of establishing the patterns that will shape the rest of our lives. A kid who grows up getting drunk every weekend or having a drink whenever he or she feels insecure can quickly develop a pattern that affects the rest of his or her life.

I'm not saying that everyone does that, and neither is the law. The law is there to protect the people who would start a harmful pattern before they understand what they're doing.

Now, the lack of patience is one of my worst qualities. But I can understand that if everyone did wait until he or she was twenty-one to drink, then there would be a lot fewer drinkers, and those who did choose to drink would be a lot more responsible. Fewer people would be getting smashed and becoming alcoholics, and fewer people would be getting killed by people who thought that they could drink and drive!

If this doesn't make sense, then go look at the drunk driving records. Look at the percentage of Americans who are alcoholics and the percentage of alcoholics who start drinking when they are teenagers. They never said, "When I grow up I want to be an alcoholic." They just started establishing a pattern of burying their problems or having a good time in a can or a bottle instead of learning how to deal with life and how to enjoy life without alcohol.

Once again, drinking is just an example here. The point is, if you're going to be able to stick by your decisions about what to do and what not to do, you're going to have to *think* about those decisions. It's not my job to tell you what the issues are and what decisions you should make. (I have enough trouble with my own decisions.) So think for yourself. Read what the Scriptures say. Understand *why* the verses are there, how to apply them, and where to get real-life examples that show the consequences. If you do that, you're less likely to be confused.

Your hands have made me and fashioned me;
Give me understanding, that I may learn Your
   commandments.

                                                    Psalm 119:73

33

God in Another Language

I was so excited last night when I got off the phone with Shane. Somehow I had begun to relate to him at his level—to reach him where he was.

It is hard sometimes for Christians to talk to non-Christians. You cannot speak to someone who has never been to church the same way you can talk to someone who grew up at church. It's almost like you're speaking two different languages!

Anyway, Shane and I were talking about God, and Shane was quite interested in what it means to have faith in Christ. So I tried to explain it the best way I could. I told him that Christ claimed to be God and proved it by coming back to life after being dead for three days. I explained how our sin separates us from God and how nothing we do can change that because God requires perfection and only Christ is perfect. Then I explained that I am trusting what Christ did on the cross to bring me back to God and to erase my sins and to give me eternal life. And Shane could understand all of this part in his own way.

But then I tried to explain to Shane how I really am a different person in Christ, how He lives in me, and how I have a growing relationship with the God who created us. I tried to communicate that this is not some imaginary story I made up to

comfort me on lonely days, but it is the root of my being and happiness. And at that point Shane started feeling a little lost and overwhelmed.

I was frustrated because I could not explain to him what mattered most in my life. So I thought to myself, *What matters the most in Shane's life right now? What can he understand best?* I realized that it was definitely his drugs.

Now, I do *not* think drugs are okay, but I knew that was where Shane was coming from. So I asked, "Shane, you know how many times I've asked you what dropping acid is like? You know how many times you have explained it to me and told me every tiny detail you could remember?"

And Shane was like, "Yeah, so what?"

I went on, "Well, no matter how many times you describe it or how hard I try to understand, the answer you give me will *never* be complete because I have never tried it. Unless I try acid for myself, I will never know what it is like. I mean, you tell me you feel like you are melting. I have no idea, or at least only a vague idea, of what it feels like to melt. (No, Shane, I don't want to feel like that. I'm just trying to make a point.)

"Well, Shane, that's how it is for me when I *try* to explain what it's like to have God and Christ in me. I can explain how I talk to Him, how I now have the choice to do right instead of being trapped in my old patterns, how my love for Him deepens, and how I am in an intimate and close relationship that is constantly growing. But you will not catch a glimpse of what I am saying until you try God for yourself. Talk about expanding your brain and intellect . . . God will give you a new perspective on everything!

"I can give you the proof through historians that Jesus was a real man in history. He was crucified under the regional governor Pontius Pilate, and more than two hundred people claimed to see Him alive three days later. The stone that was covering His tomb was rolled away, and the body was not there. It was never found anywhere else. The facts are plain and real, and there is nonbiased evidence to support them.

"But, Shane, I think you know this; I think you know the truth. If you don't, then ask God to show you the truth. He'll do it if you ask Him."

As I continue to pray for Shane, I think about a verse I learned in Ephesians, where the apostle Paul prays that God will give someone else "the spirit of wisdom and revelation in the knowledge of Him" (Ephesians 1:17). If you don't know Christ in a personal way, I pray that for you, too.

> **Making mention of you in my prayers: that the God of our Lord Jesus Christ, the Father of glory, may give to you the spirit of wisdom and revelation in the knowledge of Him, the eyes of your understanding being enlightened; that you may know what is the hope of His calling, what are the riches of the glory of His inheritance in the saints, and what is the exceeding greatness of His power toward us who believe.**
> **Ephesians 1:16–19**

34

I Don't Understand!

*D*ear God, I'm really mad at You! Why are You letting this happen to me?

"I finally met people who love You and who understand me—people I can open up to. They are not fanatical "Bible beaters" I can't relate to; they're cool. I can go snowboarding with them, enjoy decent movies with them, and talk with them about anything.

"I've been praying so long for this kind of friends, and I've finally found them. So now my parents are saying we have to move . . . to *Oklahoma!* That's half a country away, and I don't know anyone there.

"What's the deal here, God? Why is my world falling in, just when I thought it was coming together? Have I done something wrong? Is this my fault?

"God, are You even listening? . . ."

Sometimes it is so hard to trust God! Like Suzanne, who had to move when things were coming together for her, we can get frustrated when we want something so badly and it doesn't work out.

You save your money for months to go skiing and then get the flu the day before you're supposed to leave. Or you finally manage to find your own apartment, but your roommate bails out and you can't afford the rent. Or your mom and dad go through a year of counseling and still decide to get a divorce.

And all you can say is "Why, God? I don't understand!"

Sometimes that's just the way it is. Sometimes things happen, and we can't understand why; we have to trust God that things will work out. Sure, we can look for answers. In fact, I think God *wants* us to use our minds and try to understand. Often the reasons are not clear, but God still wants us to obey Him.

And obedience isn't easy. A lot of times it hurts to follow God, especially when we don't have a clue what's going on.

But it helps to remember that God isn't out to get us . . . even when it seems like He is. God made us. He knows our needs even better than we do, and He always wants what is best for us. And He wants us to come to Him with our problems, even our frustration and anger toward Him. He can take it.

When things happen that you can't understand, don't stop talking to God. Be honest about your feelings. If you don't, your anger will grow and will distance you from God and others who really love you.

Ask God to show you why He has allowed certain circumstances and what you are supposed to learn from them. Go to other Christians, too, and ask what they do to get through tough times. Finally, ask God to help you be content with where you are and with what He has given you.

Whatever you do, don't just sit there and be frustrated. Go to God. Tell Him how you feel. He can take it. And He loves you more than you can ever understand.

My God, My God, why have You forsaken Me?
Why are You so far from helping Me,
And from the words of My groaning?
O My God, I cry in the daytime, but You do not hear;
And in the night season, and am not silent.

But You are holy . . .
Our fathers trusted in You;
They trusted, and You delivered them.

Psalm 22:1–4

35

No More Separation

a young girl sits on the steps of her camp cabin writing a letter home. Other kids are swimming and canoeing, but she's so homesick she even misses her little brother.

A teenager lies on the bed in her room. She can't stop crying, even though it's been more than a week since she had that big fight with her boyfriend. She can't even remember what the fight was about. She misses him so much.

Two kids sit at the front window, staring in disbelief as their father finishes loading the trunk, climbs into his car, and drives off. They had not imagined their parents would ever go through with the divorce. But now he is just . . . gone.

I think that *separation* is one of the ugliest words in the English language! It hurts so much to be cut off from the people you love, the people you need, and the people who care about you.

Little babies scream when they are separated from their moms, and moms panic when they can't find their little ones. Best friends feel lost if they are separated from the person they spend the most time with. Boyfriends and girlfriends long for each other when they are apart. And the hurt is much deeper for married people who have to be separated. They have become one in every aspect of their lives; they are a part of each other. When they are separated, they feel like a part of them is missing.

Well, if you can imagine it, God's love is deeper than that of a mother and child, deeper than the closest friends, deeper than the love of a man and a woman. When we have trust in what Christ did—His death and resurrection—to save us, then the Holy Spirit comes and lives inside us. He comes into our lives and will never leave us. Even if our friends and family reject or abandon us, God *never* will no matter what we do. When God makes a promise and a commitment, He does not back out of it.

Unfortunately, people aren't that trustworthy. In fact, I think one reason people feel unstable about trusting God is because they have seen so many examples of broken promises, broken relationships, and broken commitments. They have a hard time imagining what true commitment is. They live in fear of being let down and abandoned. That's why it is so incredible to know that, no matter what people have done, God is never going to leave us. He doesn't threaten us by saying, "If you do that one more time, then I'm out of here!"

You may be asking, "If all that is true, then why do I feel so distant from God sometimes? Why do I feel like God has deserted me?"

There are lots of possible reasons, but one is that *you* may be the one who is distancing yourself from God, not the other way around.

God is always reaching out to us, loving us and forgiving us through Christ. When we depend on that, understanding and accepting God's forgiveness, and look to Him and serve Him, then we are facing our Creator in a warm embrace. But when we choose to sin, we are choosing to turn our backs on Him. So we feel separated. God is still there with His arms open wide, but there we stand too proud to confess our sins and run into His embrace and feel His perfect forgiveness.

I think that is a big part of the pain we feel when we sin. It's not just guilt or the natural consequences of the sin itself. The biggest pain is the pain of separation, knowing that we're not with the one we love. It's like when a boyfriend and girlfriend have a big fight. They're both miserable because the separation hurts so much. Well, the deeper my relationship becomes with God, the more painful it becomes to separate from Him, so I desire to obey Him more.

I think that this is what makes a mature Christian. It's not that he or she walks around with a list of rules that must be followed in order to be a good Christian. It's that his or her love has grown so great for God that he or she doesn't want to be separated from Him.

If you still feel separated from God, do not think that you are a horrible Christian for feeling that way. Sometimes the pain we feel when others leave us transfers to how we think God is. Don't believe it. Feelings will come and go. God will not. He is here to stay!

For I am persuaded that neither death nor life, nor angels nor principalities nor powers, nor things present nor things to come, nor height nor depth, nor any other created thing, shall be able to separate us from the love of God which is in Christ Jesus our Lord.
Romans 8:38–39

36

No Emotions

ristie grew up next door to an older girl named Rose, who was like a big sister to her. Rose was different from the other people Kristie knew because she was so honest. If Kristie talked to Rose about a problem, she would never tell Kristie to just smile and trust God. Rose seemed to understand hurt and loneliness. She would remind Kristie of God's love, but she would also confirm that there is real sin and pain in this world that is not going to go away until we get to heaven.

Rose was the only Christian Kristie knew who seemed to give her real answers. That is why Kristie was so devastated when Rose was killed in a car accident. She could not believe it had really happened, and she felt like she would never stop crying.

But the other Christians Kristie talked to did not understand. They said, "Why are you crying? Don't you know that Rose is in heaven now? You should be rejoicing for her!" But that didn't help at all. Kristie was hurting, and she needed comfort. She had to work through her pain and grief with God, which she could do because Rose had shown her how by being so honest with her about God.

Why are so many of us taught to have no emotions, worries, problems, or hurts? It is especially hard for guys in this world to show, or admit, that they are hurt. I think, in some situations, it is even more difficult for Christian guys to show emotion.

Why is it that once you step on the campus of a Christian college or high school you are expected to be smiling all the time? Does being Christian mean we do not feel pain? That's ridiculous! Paul warned us not to be surprised when painful trials come our way. And Jesus wept when his friend Lazarus died. Why do we so often overlook that?

I think that many Christians just aren't facing reality. I mean, how are you supposed to react when a friend dies and then some Christian says something like, "Why are you crying? She's in heaven . . . you are being selfish to worry about yourself." Or, "You know, it was just God's will."

Do you really think it is God's plan for someone to go to some party, get drunk, and then crash into another person while driving home from her friend's house? Sure, God allows it to happen. He gives us the freedom to follow our own will or His, and He lets the natural consequences of the world fall into place.

God allows bad things to happen, but I don't think He goes, "Who do I want to kill today?" And I *know* He does not expect us just to keep on smiling when it happens. He knows it hurts us to lose someone we love, whether it be from a death, a break-up, a move, or a divorce.

So when you are hurting, let yourself cry. That's what Jesus did. And then go to people who will sit in silence or cry with you! We are not God's robots with buttons we can push to turn off a bad feeling! We are His children whom He loves and has compassion for. And He tells us that we should have compassion, too! Part of following the great command to love our neighbor is to mourn for them when they leave us. So cry, let it out—and pray for someone to understand you or comfort you.

If you believe the lie that God does not want you to show any emotions, it is going to be difficult for you to have a deep relationship with God. You also will have a more shallow relationship with Him because you won't be honest with Him. You'll be hiding your true confusion, bewilderment, pain, and anger when He wants to embrace you and comfort you and eventually heal your open wounds.

I can't express in words how much God loves you, and how He hurts when you hurt. His Son has been here and has felt the pain of loneliness, rejection, loss, and anger. He prayed so honestly and earnestly to His Father that He sweat blood. He died to forgive the people who take advantage of us, hurt us, infect innocent people with AIDS, drive drunk, commit adultery, divorce, murder, slander, lie. He died for all of us, and He knows the pain of complete separation brought on by death.

So when you hurt, run to Him! He won't immediately take away the tears, but He will be with you feeling your hurt and leading you toward more trust in Him—and more strength to endure what's ahead!

Now when Job's three friends heard of all this adversity that had come upon him, each one came from his own place. . . . They lifted their voices and wept; and each one tore his robe and sprinkled dust on his head toward heaven. So they sat down with him on the ground seven days and seven nights . . . for they saw that his grief was very great.

Job 2:11–13

37

God's Friend

The more I grow and the more I learn, the more amazed I am by the beauty and complexity of this universe God made.

For instance, it is amazing to study science and see how men and women like Galileo and Curie and Einstein could peer through telescopes and microscopes and understand God in a deeper way. After all, it was God who created stars and microbes and elements and energy.

It is great to read English literature and see the beauty and wisdom that people like Emily Dickinson, Dostoyevsky, J. R. R. Tolkien, Madeleine L'engle, and C. S. Lewis could create in stories, poems, and novels. Realizing that God created each one of those authors shows me how vast God's knowledge is.

It is fascinating to study psychology, which is the study of human behavior. When I see how complex human thought and behavior are, I am amazed that God could dream it all up!

And it is especially exciting to study the Bible and to understand I am free in Christ. I do not need to hide from the world God made. I do not need to hide my feelings of anger, pain, insecurity, or confusion. I do not need to deny my sexuality and act like I have no sexual desires in order to remain sexually pure. All these things are part of who I am . . . a person God made.

I love learning about all these things that God created—His

work, His people, His music, the creativity He places in humans, and His creative universe. But what I enjoy most about God is that I can have a friendship with Him for eternity. I can actually be friends with the amazing, fascinating, and exciting Creator of the universe.

It's great to be able to call God and know He is *always* there. God's not busy, watching some TV program while I am trying to talk to Him. His mind isn't on something else when I need Him. He's listening to me, loving me, caring for me, and taking care of all of my needs.

I don't have to worry about limiting my time with God. I can talk to Him no matter where I am or what I am doing. I can write Him a letter and I can know that He is responding to it. I can turn to His Word and read it and be encouraged. I can pull out a CD and hear all about God's love.

I can go to church and hear God's Word being applied, and I can talk to people my age who can tell me how God is changing their lives. I can go outside and see God's beauty. I can sing to Him. I never have to be separated from God.

Of course, I need to have a balanced life. I mean, it is not good for me to sit in my room and read my Bible and listen to music twenty-four hours a day. God wants me to open up and spend time with other people. He wants me to live life and understand how to relate to other Christians, as well as non-Christians. But as I go through the day, I can know whether I am alone or with others, I can always turn to Jesus. He is a trusted friend.

No longer do I call you servants, for a servant does not know what his master is doing; but I have called you friends, for all things that I heard from My Father I have made known to you.

John 15:15

38

Only One Way? Why?

*N*onbeliever: "The problem with your religion is simple. You keep insisting that the only way to get to heaven is through Christ."

Believer: "What's the problem with that?"

Nonbeliever: "I'll tell you what's wrong . . . it's rude! I mean, who wants to convert to some religion that tells me all of my friends are going to be in hell. Besides, don't you think you're being a little conceited to say that your religion is the only right one?"

Believer: "Well, no, because I have no reason to be conceited. Jesus is the one who said He is the only way to get to heaven (John 14:6). I believed Him and accepted His gift of forgiveness."

Nonbeliever: "But how do you *know* that Jesus is who He said He is . . . and why would there only be one way?"

Believer: "Well, there are a lot of reasons why I believe. For one thing, Jesus' death is historically documented more than any other burial. He rose three days later to prove that He is the Son of the living God.

"To answer your other question, I do not know how there can be many ways to get to heaven. How can fifteen different religions that contradict each other all get you to the same end? There is only one answer to the problem of two plus two. It always equals four. Three or five might be closer to the answer of four than nine is, but four is the only right answer."

Nonbeliever: "Well, if Jesus is the only way, then why are there so many people out there who are not Christians, but still lead good lives by being good citizens, being kind to other people, and stuff like that?"

Believer: "Well, I cannot answer for everyone else, but I know that Christianity is distinctly different from all the other religions in that it is the only one that does not say that people must work for or earn their salvation. I try to do what is right because I believe that God is our Creator. His way is the truth. I love Him and I want to please Him. I want to follow the truth, not a lie."

Nonbeliever: "Oh, no . . . you think that God is the Creator of the world? You believe in that Adam and Eve stuff?"

Believer: "Uh-huh, I do."

Nonbeliever: "What about the theories of evolution?"

Believer: "Well, some of my ideas have been stated better by C. S. Lewis. He said that if the world was formed by accidental chance, if plants evolved into animals, into monkeys, into us—thinking human beings—which isn't really logical in the first place, then something would have to come from nothing. It's like saying that milk could produce a cow by accident someday. Anyway, if we were formed by chance, then all of these thoughts are accidents. The people who believe in this theory of evolution are mere accidents themselves. So why should I believe what an 'accident' is trying to say to me about his theories of this evolving universe? I really don't want to sound rude, but I think it is more difficult to believe in an accident than in a Creator God who sent His Son to show us what we probably should have already known."

Nonbeliever: "This is getting ridiculous! I don't think I even want to hear anymore."

Believer: "That's fine; I'm sorry. I didn't mean to make you mad."

Nonbeliever: "No, I'm just sick of this topic. Why does it always come up?"

I am not claiming to have all the answers, you guys. I'm just convinced that God wants us to be bold and to know *why* we believe what we believe. I think that from the day you become a Christian on you should be able to explain why you accepted Christ. You do not necessarily have to have books of knowledge to tell someone about Christ. But the more you study the historical facts about Christ, and the more you look into the other religions and see why they are not true, then the more your faith will be reaffirmed and the more effectively you will be able discuss your faith with other people who doubt.

I believe, as C. S. Lewis expressed, that our faith is not—or should not be—based on feelings. The feelings overflow from the facts that we know to be true! Find out what they are!

> **But sanctify the Lord God in your hearts, and always be ready to give a defense to everyone who asks you a reason for the hope that is in you, with meekness and fear.**
>
> **1 Peter 3:15**

39

God,
Is This Love?

$\mathcal{A}$nna had been casually dating people since high school. She liked many of the guys she went out with and even developed some crushes, but she never found the right person. In fact, by her junior year in college she had reached the point that guys weren't her focus anymore. She had her friends and her studies, and she wasn't that interested in getting serious with a guy.

Then one night Anna went out with a group of friends and she ended up talking with this guy from another school. She had met him a few times before, but had never thought anything could come out of it. Well, this night was different! She and Matt seemed to be laughing about everything. She stayed up late that night and talked to him for a long time.

Anna was still skeptical about things working out for her and Matt because other relationships had not worked out for her in the past. But this felt so different! Anna spent hours talking to and listening to Matt. She felt so natural around him. For the first time she felt she was allowed to be herself with a guy. She could tell him when she was scared about something. She could tell him when she was feeling hurt or pushed away. He seemed to care about her and listened to her talk about her doubts about people and life.

This was a new experience for Anna. She thought back on

crushes she had had before, and she never wanted that kind of love again. She knew she was getting closer to the real thing . . . what God intended love to be. She just hadn't known that there could be so much life and happiness in this act of loving another person and being loved.

The next few months were wonderful. Anna and Matt got really close quickly; they never wanted to be separated from each other. Schoolwork was secondary. There wasn't much time for other friends. The whole world seemed to consist of God, Matt, and Anna. Anna remembered some books she had read in high school that said she shouldn't spend all of her time with a new guy, but she thought she knew better. "I do not want to smother Matt, but if he wants to spend the time with me, then why shouldn't we?"

Well, after a while, problems started coming up between Anna and Matt. Matt seemed frustrated, and Anna couldn't figure out why. Matt couldn't seem to explain it very well, although he tried a few times. Pretty soon it was clear that Matt was backing off. He still cared about Anna, but he felt pressured by her unspoken expectations about what a boyfriend was "supposed" to do. Eventually he started to resent her.

Anna couldn't understand exactly what was happening, but she could sense that Matt was slipping away. She was hurt, and she blamed her hurt on Matt.

Matt and Anna finally broke up. Anna was devastated. Yeah, yeah, she knew that God still loved her, and that He would not leave her, and that somehow life was going to go on. But she had never felt this much pain before in her life. She felt as if she had been torn in half. She had opened up her life to Matt; he had become her best friend. Now, he was gone.

Anna knew it was Matt's right to choose what he wanted to do; she had to let go. But what was she supposed to do now? Where was she supposed to go? In the last few months she had created distance between herself and her old friends, so now nobody seemed to be there for her. Every night she sobbed herself to sleep. She called out and wept to God. What had she done wrong? Why did loving somebody have to hurt so much?

You guys, I do not have the guide on relationships! But I know they can be wonderful, and they can be difficult. The closer and more serious you get, the more difficult they are sometimes. But I think we can learn even from our painful experiences in relationships.

If you are in a relationship right now—whether it's going well or having some problems—it might help to ask yourself a few questions:

- Am I putting God first in this relationship?
- Would I follow what God wants me to do in this relationship, or am I *more* concerned with what my boyfriend or girlfriend wants?
- Do I spend too much time with him or her?
- Do I have other close friends I can, and do, go to when I have a problem? Have I dropped my old friends since becoming involved with my boyfriend or girlfriend?
- Have I put off activities and goals that I used to think were very important?
- Am I giving the other person freedom, or am I trying to control his or her decisions?
- Am I beginning to feel angry at some of the expectations that are being put upon me?
- Is this person encouraging me and helping me to see God more clearly, or are either of us bringing each other down?
- Am I mature enough to handle a serious relationship?
- Do I respect myself enough to stand up for what I think is right and not compromise my beliefs?
- Can I see my faults and let God forgive them? Can I love the other person and forgive his or her faults, accepting this person the way he or she is?

In this world, I think it is hard to keep a healthy relationship going. But when both people are committed to God and choose to be committed to learning how to love each other, then I know it can work. And even when relationships *don't* work out, we can learn from them and apply what we learned to give other relationships a better chance.

Learning how to love someone else is one of the greatest things you can do in your life!

Love suffers long and is kind; love does not envy; love does not parade itself, is not puffed up; does not behave rudely, does not seek its own, is not provoked, thinks no evil; does not rejoice in iniquity, but rejoices in the truth; bears all things, believes all things, hopes all things, endures all things. Love never fails. . . . And now abide faith, hope, love, these three; but the greatest of these is love.

1 Corinthians 13:4–8, 13

40

This Is Gonna Hurt

at this moment I cannot tell you how much I like being a Christian in this world because, right now, I don't! I do like knowing that God is working in my life. But this world is *full* of sin, and being a Christian often hurts. It seems like people hate you when they see a part of the truth in your life that they are rebelling against, and they get mad at you for exposing their errors. So you feel persecuted at times. You are persecuted at times! Why would anybody love that?

Let's face it. Following Christ, I mean really following Him, is hard. If we do it correctly, some people will laugh at us and call us fanatics. Sometimes we feel left out, like everyone else is having fun and we're not. Sometimes we are disillusioned by the way our fellow Christians act or by the way we act. Sometimes we're lonely and tired and God seems a million miles away.

But why does any of that surprise us? After all, we've been warned! The Bible clearly tells us that if we choose to follow Christ we can expect to suffer. The apostle Peter put it this way. "Beloved, do not think it strange concerning the fiery trial which is to try you, as though some strange thing happened to you" (1 Pet. 4:12).

My favorite author, C. S. Lewis, expands on this concept by pointing out that people who do not have morals, very much like animals, do not have moral problems. Think about it. If I don't believe that honesty is important, am I going to be tormented by guilt after I have someone else to write my research paper? If I don't care about integrity or kindness, will I have any qualms about stepping all over other people to get what I want? In some ways, it would be a lot easier just not to care. But that would mean being stuck in the world without Christ's love and forgiveness.

C. S. Lewis also points out that sleeping people have no problems. But sleeping people don't really have much of a life, either. So that brings us to this verse: "Awake you who sleep,/ Arise from the dead,/ And Christ will give you light" (Eph. 5:14). Even if it hurts, if we want to experience real life in Christ, then we need to wake up and wake each other up. We need to take the risk of following Christ and doing what He says, even if that means we have to experience pain for standing up for what we know is right.

We are still going to face immense pain in this world at times, and we need to cry, hurt, and not ignore our feelings. But suffering isn't all there is in this life. God gives us so much opportunity to find joy. He has given us forgiveness, the Holy Spirit, a living hope, and heaven to look forward to. He gives us a beautiful world to explore, family to care for us, friends to enjoy, beauty to savor, knowledge to acquire, and curiosity to spur us on. And He gives us His love . . . a love that has no end.

When I stop focusing on my problems (which does not mean that I push them down and ignore them), I begin to catch a glimpse of what God really has in store for me not only in heaven, but as part of His kingdom right here in this world.

Most assuredly, I say to you that you will weep and la-ment, but the world will rejoice; and you will be sor-rowful, but your sorrow will be turned into joy. . . . In the world you will have tribulation; but be of good cheer, I have overcome the world.

John 16:20, 33

41

First Love

I remember the first time it happened; it made me so mad! (It still makes me mad remembering it.)

It was right after I had rededicated my life to Christ, and I was excited about the new love and meaning I was discovering. One day I was talking to this woman at my church about what was happening in my life, and she smiled condescendingly. "Oh, Cheryl, I know what it's like. Young Christians are always so intense, so in love with Jesus. I was like that, too. But just wait a few years; you'll mellow out."

To me, that's like telling me that I'll go out and fall in love with this wonderful guy and get married, but after a few years I won't love my husband anymore! Is that something I should look forward to or let happen?

Okay, I know that in marriage the initial excitement of being in love does quiet down. I know that a couple's relationship after twenty years is different from their relationship when they are newlyweds. But I don't believe intimate love has to vanish as so many say. After the first thrill of being in love wears off, you move on to a more mature but deeper love.

In the same way, I can't believe that growing in Christ means getting bored with being a Christian! Sure, we won't always feel that excited "high" we feel when we first come to Christ. But if our love for Him doesn't keep growing and

maturing, if it gets bored and cynical, then I think something's wrong.

Sure, there will be days when we don't feel very loving toward God, and when we can't feel His love for us. Some days we're tempted to pack our bags and leave . . . to give up on loving God. There are times when we want to say, "I just want to give in. I'm tired of fighting. That's it; I cannot take this anymore!"

The world tells us we can do it that way. If a commitment we've made, like marriage or following Christ, is not working out, the world tells us we can bail out or ignore the problems and go our own ways. The Bible says that being a Christian is a lot like marriage. But it's clear that God does not look at marriage like the world does. He is not going to bail out of our lives when we hurt Him. And He expects us to follow Him even when we don't feel like it.

Listen, please! God is not asking us to witness to ten thousand people a day, write books like C. S. Lewis, or translate the Bible into thirty different languages. God simply wants us to keep coming back to our relationship with Him and to respond, "Here I am, God."

He can use us wherever we are. We need to stop running to get out of our commitments and return to our first love—Christ. If we do, our relationship will have a chance to keep on growing to maturity.

> **You have persevered and have patience, and have labored for My name's sake and have not become weary. Nevertheless I have this against you, that you have left your first love.**
>
> **Revelation 2:3–4**

42

The Divine Contradiction

I call it the divine contradiction. How are we supposed to have self-esteem when we know, or have at least gotten terrible glimpses of, how sinful we are? How are we supposed to be confident about ourselves and love ourselves but not be cocky or selfish?

To me, it does not make sense sometimes. It's kind of like those magazine covers that feature the delicious new recipe for peanut butter fudge brownies right next to the headline "How To Drop a Dress Size in a Week." Isn't it obvious that if you make and eat the peanut butter fudge brownies, you won't be able to drop a dress size in a week! And doesn't a knowledge of my own sin kind of work against my basic self-esteem?

I think part of the trouble is that we've gotten the wrong idea about what it means to have self-esteem. We think having a good self-image means thinking we're perfect or that we're just fine the way we are, no matter how sinful. But I think a healthy self-image has more to do with knowing we're *not* perfect and then being able to go on with life.

Actually, there's nothing like trying to be perfect to make us realize how imperfect we really are. The closer we grow to God, the more we compare ourselves to Him, the more we see how

holy He is and how evil we are. Not so great for the old self-esteem, huh?

Except there's more to the story. Because we draw closer to God, we should also realize how much He values us. After all, God created us; Psalm 139:13 says that he forms us in our mothers' wombs. Even when we rejected Him, He kept trying to get us back. He loved us so much, even while we were still sinning, that He sent His only Son to die for us and pay for our sins. I don't care how many times you might have heard this—we all have heard it a billion times—but think about what that truly means! If God loves and values us so much, how can we help but have self-esteem?

Developing a healthy self-image is not about being a better Christian by doing everything right and following every law perfectly. It is about grace. It's about humbling ourselves, opening the doors, and letting God's perfect healing grace shine down on us.

Why do you think it is that at our lowest points and in our deepest sorrows we begin to see how strong and true God's love is? I think it's because often that's when we start to get honest about our own imperfection. When we feel the weight of our sin so much that we cannot stand anymore, that is when most of us come before God and ask Him to forgive us and take our burdens off. That is when we experience God's awesome love and grace the most. He knows everything there is to know about us, and He still promises never to leave us or to turn His back on us.

A good self-image does not mean thinking you never do wrong. It means knowing that you do sin, that you are forgiven, and that by God's cleansing grace and power you have the strength to go on and keep trying to follow Him.

God loves you. He wants what is best for you. He will never neglect or abandon you! There's no contradiction there.

Not that I have already obtained all this, or have already been made perfect, but I press on to take hold of that for which Christ Jesus took hold of me. . . . Forgetting what is behind and straining toward what is ahead.

Philippians 3:12–13 (NIV)

43

The Kitchen Table

*I*t's a Saturday night. Nobody has a date. We're too broke for the movies and besides, we've seen all the good ones. Going to the video store sounds like too much effort, and nothing decent is on TV. But my brother and a couple of friends and I are okay; we sit around the kitchen table and talk.

Sounds boring, huh? But it's really not! In fact, the times I remember best are evenings like that. I mean, I don't remember a lot of movies I've seen with my friends. I don't have all these warm memories of hours spent with my family in front of the TV. But those times around the table were great!

Most of us these days are so caught up in *doing* something all the time. We're always trying to be entertained. When we're with our friends, we spend all our time going to movies or concerts or watching TV. And there's nothing wrong with any of these if discernment is used.

But sometimes I wonder, *Don't people ever talk anymore?* I don't mean a little in the car on the way to the movies or a quick word during commercials. I mean really talking, sharing our thoughts and ideas and feelings.

Of course, we didn't always stay at the kitchen table when we talked. Sometimes we would lie out on the back porch staring at the stars and talk until the middle of the night.

Sometimes we would walk and talk. But it wasn't a fake sort of conversation like you see in movies or have at superficial social gatherings. We talked about who we were and what we believed and what was important to us. And as we talked, we built trust and learned to love each other in a way that was genuine.

With this kind of love we could encourage each other, confront each other, laugh with and enjoy each other's company. They saw me when I would be a little brat and have my temper tantrums, but they learned to look beyond that into who I was. They did not act like I was a perfect Christian, but realized I was, and am, a forgiven Christian.

So what am I saying? I am saying that we need to take time for each other. Seriously. When is the last time you spent any time with someone who actually listened to you and cared about what you were saying? When is the last time you listened to someone else?

If you have someone you can talk to . . . someone who seems to understand you . . . then thank God. I mean it! Close friends like that are one of His best gifts. I have had too few of them in my lifetime, and right now most of them live in different states. If you don't have close friends, then pray that God will bring them to you. But don't just sit there and wait for it to happen. Pray that He will help you reach out to people and get to know them.

I challenge you that if you have close friends, regular friends, or even just acquaintances, make time for them. Plan to do something together where you are interacting, not just watching something together. Have dinner at someone's house together. Go walking somewhere; go build a fire on the beach. (Maybe stuff like that sounds fake or unrealistic, but that's because you're not used to thinking this way.)

You can even do stuff like that with your family, or even (I'm not kidding) with just your parents. Think about how weird it would be to sit at an empty table with just your dad or mom and talk. No food, no TV, no brothers and sisters, no distractions. No arguments. No lectures. Just talk about what is on your mind. Maybe it happens in your family. Maybe you could make it happen.

They really are the best times . . . canoeing down a river with my good friend, sitting at the kitchen table sharing my views and listening to other people's views, laughing and playing pool. And they can happen if we make time to relax, ease up, enjoy life, enjoy God, enjoy people, and get to know people and God on a deeper and closer level.

Every day they continued to meet together . . . in their homes and ate together with glad and sincere hearts, praising God and enjoying the favor of all the people.
Acts 2:46–47 (NIV)

44

"Safe" Sex

*a*n investigative journalist named Danny Korem once told me that sexual conflicts and sexually transmitted diseases will be the worst problem that the next generations are going to have to face. That's not hard to believe if you pay attention to the news or watch TV shows and movies. Sometimes it seems as if everything we see and hear is designed to pressure us into having sex *now!*

I think a big part of the problem is that people are masking the truth about sex. It's being portrayed sort of like a big roller coaster. "If you enjoy it and it brings you pleasure, then go ahead; but make sure to use safety precautions and follow the rules," they say. "If you're going to have sex, be sure to use a condom and have 'safe' sex."

But would you ride a roller coaster that goes upside down if someone told you that one out of every six to eight seats doesn't have a seat belt? Well, that is what "safe" sex is like. Condoms fail one out of six to eight times, and I will almost guarantee that if you have had sex, or decide to have sex, you are probably going to have it more than six times before you are married. Lots of people get pregnant with condoms, and the AIDS virus is much smaller than sperm. So it is obvious that people can, and do, get AIDS with a condom.

But I don't think that fear of pregnancy or AIDS should be what keeps you from having sex outside of marriage. If that

were the only thing stopping me, I'd probably be just like the rest of the people saying, "It will never happen to me!"

Something to consider is why God has told us to wait until marriage. If I'm serious about following Christ, I need to pay attention to what He says. And the Bible is pretty clear that sex is for marriage. But I don't think God is trying to make things hard on us by telling us to wait! God loves us, and He knows what's best for us. All His rules, including the ones about sex, are designed to make our lives better, not worse.

When two people have sex it is not just a physical act, like working out. You give a part of yourself to your partner every time you have sex. That's God's way of helping a married couple build the intimacy they need to build a life together. But having sex too soon or in the wrong context can mess up that plan. It can give you a false sense of intimacy and distract you from getting to know your partner deeply in other areas. It can make you attached to someone who is not right for you, and the memories can make it hard to build intimacy later in marriage. (If you *do* think true intimacy is there—intellectually, emotionally, and spiritually—then what is stopping you from being married?)

I believe that if I wait, then my marriage will have a stronger foundation because it will not be based just on sex. Plus, my husband and I will be able to trust each other and be completely vulnerable with each other without having to wonder who the other person has been with.

And the way I look at it, if my future husband and I are going to be having sex for the rest of our lives, why do I need to go around from person to person now? Sex is a gift from God, like walking or running. Anyone can learn to do it right when the time comes. I don't need to practice now to "get ready."

So there are a bunch of reasons, besides fear of AIDS and pregnancy, not to have sex outside of marriage. And no matter what people tell you or what you see on TV, it is possible to be a fairly well-adjusted person without having sex. And it is

possible to have self-control and resist sexual temptation. God gives us a free will, He gives us the ability to make a choice about what we are going to do. He has promised he won't let us be tempted beyond what we can bear (1 Cor. 10:13). And He can give us the strength and the freedom to choose what is best for us—to learn how to respect ourselves and others.

But we have to cooperate. We have to think about this issue, be completely honest with ourselves, and make our own choices—that means that if we get to a point where we think there is no going back, we get out of there fast! It means we have to make limits for ourselves and make a decision not to get to that point again. We also have the responsibility to be open and honest with the person we're dating.

All this is not to say that having sex outside of marriage is the unpardonable sin. God can forgive us and heal us wherever we are and for whatever we have done. But it's important not to use that statement as an excuse for not obeying Him. He has made it clear that the *only* safe sex is sex within a monogamous relationship . . . a strong, trusting marriage.

For you, brethren, have been called to liberty; only do not use liberty as an opportunity for the flesh, but through love serve one another. . . . Walk in the Spirit, and you shall not fulfill the lust of the flesh.
Galatians 5:13, 16

45

Go to
the Source

"My pastor is always right!"

Wrong!

Okay, I don't even know your pastor. But I do know that no human being on this earth gets it right all the time.

Think of it this way. You and your sister get into a big fight about something. You run to your parents to tell on one another. Both of you have a different story about what happened. You can sit and listen to what your sister says and think, *How in the world did she come up with that story?* And she could listen to you explain the fight and be bewildered by your excuses. There is probably some truth in what both of you are saying, but both of you are also probably wrong.

We live in a fallen world. Everybody has his or her own way of looking at things. And anybody can be wrong. Even parents. Even teachers. Even pastors.

It is not necessarily that someone wants to preach a lie. It is just that preachers sometimes take Scriptures out of context to support what they want it to say (just like you usually cover the way you saw the fight and your sister talks about her side). Sometimes this twisting of the Scriptures is done intentionally, and sometimes it is done by habit or by accident.

If you stop to think for a second, you could probably think

of lots of people who took Scriptures out of context! Satan certainly did! When Jesus was in the wilderness for forty days, Satan came and tempted Him by quoting Scripture and twisting the meaning for his own purpose. Satan did the same thing when he was talking to Eve in the Garden of Eden. Look in Genesis and see how he persuaded Eve by twisting God's words.

Does it surprise you that Satan knows the Bible so well? It kind of surprises me when I think about it. But should it surprise you when a member of a religious cult seems to know the Bible inside out? We really need to study the Scriptures and *know* them, or we could be persuaded by nice-sounding "religious" words and phrases that are lies.

That's one reason I think it's good for you to know that a teenager is writing this. I have been intimidated by people who are older than I am, who appear to be very wise and full of knowledge. Sometimes they use big words and phrases that I cannot even understand. And my automatic response is, "They know what they are talking about." Not necessarily.

I mean, right now there are adults saying that the phrase, "My grace is sufficient for even thee" means that we should not ever see a psychologist or even a family doctor. Some people have taken the phrase, "For what fellowship does light have with darkness" to mean we should not marry interracially. Some people say that Jesus was not a real person with flesh but only a spirit. I've heard people say that God had sex with the Virgin Mary to have Jesus. One pastor was even trying to tell me that John the Baptist did not baptize anyone! I have come to believe that all of these interpretations are wrong, but when they are surrounded by all sorts of nice bits of evidence, then it is sometimes difficult to determine. (Obviously, in giving these examples I'm giving my own version of the truth. Study and think for yourself and use your judgment.)

All this means that you can't just accept the things people tell you, even people in authority like pastors and teachers. I don't mean you have to rebel and challenge them all the time, but there's nothing wrong with asking honest questions. No matter what, you do need to listen and study with an active brain. If I were you I would start now. In college you cannot simply not take a class because you do not want to hear lies. You have to apply your brain and study hard.

Try to determine what is fact and what is theory. Even books can be wrong or biased. It's up to you to learn from the good and weed out the bad. (I have had some science teachers who believed in evolution. I don't. Yet I have still learned some very useful scientific facts and procedures from these teachers.)

In church you need to have an active mind too. You will want to know your Scripture—so that you can check if what the pastor is saying agrees or disagrees with the Word. A good pastor will *want* you to do this.

It gets confusing and frustrating sometimes when your pastor says one thing, your parents say another, you think yet another way, and then the Scriptures clearly go against all three! Who wins? Well, I'd definitely say God's Word does. But you are going to have to decide sooner or later whether to trust the Bible for all your ultimate decisions or not.

> **But evil men and impostors will grow worse and worse, deceiving and being deceived. But you must continue in the things which you have learned and been assured of, knowing . . . that from childhood you have known the Holy Scriptures.**
> **2 Timothy 3:13–15**

46

Everywhere I Go

Wouldn't it be awesome if we could see Jesus everywhere we went?

Imagine it. It's your first day in a new school. You walk down the hall through a river of unfamiliar faces. Without realizing it, you're stretching your neck hoping to spot one person you recognize, even though you know there won't be anybody. And then, all of a sudden you see Jesus, standing right there waving His arms for you to come sit with Him.

For some reason I don't think if Jesus were here in the flesh that He would be like any of the adults we know. Our parents and teachers seem to forget what it is like to be young. They laugh at things we do not find funny and get mad at us for not understanding them all of the time. But Jesus knows everything. And that means He does not forget what a teenager is like. He used to be a teenager Himself.

I cannot picture Jesus saying words like *radical, awesome,* and *dork* in the wrong context! I do not think Jesus would even try to use those words like many adults do (somehow they think we can understand them better when they keep on repeating our phrases).

Anyway, the point is that Jesus really *is* here! If we are Christians, He lives in us. I am sure you already know that, and the last thing I want to do is repeat facts you have heard a

million times. But what does it mean, really, to have Christ living in us?

One thing it means is He is never far away when we need Him. Once when I was at a new high school, I got so lonely on one of my breaks that I walked to a secluded place so I could cry. When I was all alone, I prayed aloud, "Jesus, can You see me? Do You hear me? Do You even care that I am here by myself?"

I sat there for ten minutes in complete silence. And all of a sudden this song came up in my head; a song I had not sung in a long time. It is from Psalm 3:3.

> But You, O LORD, are a shield for me,
> My glory and the One who lifts up my head.

And suddenly I knew in my heart that Jesus was standing right next to me.

I am not a crazy person! And I'm here to tell you that Jesus answered my prayer with that one verse that I sang as a child. When I was hurting and alone, Jesus reminded me of His promise to protect me and be with me.

That does not mean I smiled and skipped off to my next class. Let's be realistic here! It means that I wiped my tears and made myself go to my next class with all my fears and lonely feelings. I was only able to do that because Jesus reassured me of His love, and He reminded me that I need to go on in order to bring glory to Him.

Jesus really is there in the middle of our lives. Just think of him standing there in the middle of all of the people at a sporting event of some kind, or in the crowd at your first school formal, or in your new house in a foreign city. When you are down or lonely, think of Jesus right beside you . . . picking you up, listening to you, loving you, encouraging you, disciplining you . . . all in a way that only He knows how.

Even though you have fallen and gotten bruised so many

times you can't remember, there He is right beside you to pick you up and comfort you and help you get started again. Doesn't it change things to know you are running with someone who loves you so much He traded His life for yours? Isn't it great to realize you are being supported and carried by the One you so clumsily have been trying to follow?

And then you suddenly understand that not only is Jesus running with you, but He's also waiting for you at the end of the race. There He stands with arms outstretched, waiting for you to run into them.

The race isn't over yet. You have a long way to go. But Jesus is with you now, and He's waiting for you at the end. No matter what happens, things are going to be all right.

And lo, I am with you *always,* **even to the end of the age.**

Matthew 28:20

47

Surprise! Surprise! Surprise!

hy am I so surprised when God answers my prayers? I have been looking through some of my old journals and notes, and I found prayers like:

"Lord God, please make me totally dependent on you. . . ."

"God, help me to do everything for your glory. . . ."

"Teach me patience and humility. . . ."

Now, those are some scary prayers! Was I thinking when I let them out of my mouth and actually wrote them down? I didn't know what I was getting into, so maybe I should warn you. Be careful how you pray.

After all, God is the Creator of the universe. He made all things and all people. He can do anything that He wants to do—including answering any prayers we send His way.

God wants to answer our prayers, too. No, that doesn't mean that He's dying to give us that red Porsche we want to impress our friends with. But God wants us to become more like Christ; He showed us that through the words and examples of His Son. So if we pray for Christ-like qualities like patience and trust and dependence on God, then God won't turn His head. If He tells us to ask for something, and we do ask for it, He is going to come through for us.

Which brings us back to the fact that we should be careful how we pray, especially if we pray to be more like Christ The thing is, God will answer our prayers, but we might not like the way He does it. Learning to be patient, for example, can be very difficult and painful. (That seems to be the prayer request God is never slow at answering.) And you'd better watch out when you pray for self-control and diligence.

When I prayed for God to show me how to be more dependent on Him, I guess I expected Him to just inject the quality into me, like a supernatural vaccination. I had no idea He would teach me through painful circumstances in my life, like having to move away from all of my friends and school, having to lose a beloved friend in a car accident, having to remain single because I only want to date Christians, and having a best friend move.

Maybe it was the only way He could get me to listen. I mean, I kept on clinging to my friends, my sports, and my possessions to make me happy. I kept depending on those things, yet I somehow seemed to keep on blurting out my prayers for God to change me. So why was I so surprised when God started prying my clinging fingers off of the things I was holding on to? Why was I so devastated when I started to lose all of these things one by one?

Now, don't misunderstand me. I am not saying we must give up all of our worldly possessions and our friends to become closer to God. I don't think we have to inflict pain on ourselves to follow Him; we'll have enough pain in life as it is. I also don't believe that God sits around thinking of ways to zap us just to make sure we're dependent on Him. But I do think He uses what happens in our lives, especially the painful things, to help us see the truth about ourselves and our relationship to Him.

I think, from reading Scripture, that we are supposed to look at the people and things in our lives as gifts. The problems come when we start thinking we have earned them, or when we base self-worth on these things and become dependent on them instead of on God. That's when we need to learn some hard lessons about who or what comes first in our lives.

Why do you think God asked Abraham to sacrifice his son Isaac? God was working on Abraham's character and teaching him how to be dependent on God. I would not be surprised to hear that at some point in his life Abraham had prayed that same prayer that I prayed.

And do you think Abraham wanted to kill his only son, the boy he had waited for most of his life and finally received in his old age? Of course not! I do not think when Abraham got his orders to sacrifice Isaac that he smiled and said, "Great idea, God, I'll get right to it!" But he did respond with faith, believing that God knows best, and following Him out of obedience. And in that experience, Abraham learned something about how to trust God and depend upon Him. I am trying hard to learn the same lesson.

I don't know why I keep clinging to the gifts God gives to me (or loans to me). I do wish I could learn how to be dependent on Him without all of this pain. I wish I could learn how to be humble without constantly falling on my face because I did it *my* way. (Maybe I need to pray to be a quicker learner!)

I am warning you to be careful when you pray, "God, help me to love my enemies, respect my parents, and follow You completely." God is able and willing to answer your prayers, but the learning process may be painful. So pray for endurance and for the courage to work through the pain. Ask God to help you see that we are only here for a few moments in comparison to eternity. And when things are hard, remember to ask, "God, what are You trying to teach me? I want to learn!"

Beloved, do not think it strange concerning the fiery trial which is to try you, as though some strange thing

happened to you; but rejoice to the extent that you partake of Christ's sufferings, that when His glory is revealed, you may also be glad with exceeding joy.

1 Peter 4:12–13

48

This Is College?

*J*ustin didn't know what was wrong with him. He had thought he would love college, but now he seemed to be freaking out. Everything was unfamiliar to him. The campus seemed huge; there was no way he was going to find his classes.

Not that his classes were all that great, anyway! He had to wait hours to register, and because he was a freshman he was not given priority for classes. Most of the classes he wanted were already taken by juniors and seniors.

After Justin registered he decided he had to get his books. That line was only a mile long, too. Everywhere he went there seemed to be long lines, hidden expenses, and papers to get signed by advisers and professors. He did not know anyone or how to get anywhere. *This is college,* Justin thought. He wanted to disappear, and on this big campus it didn't seem like it was going to be too difficult.

Justin buried himself in his room with his books and his computer. He would leave only to go to his classes and to eat. Soon he found it uncomfortable even to go to the cafeteria. It was always full of people, and everybody seemed to have his or her own group to hang out with. Why did he feel like everybody was looking at him? He began to panic and did not have a clue as to what he was supposed to do.

Was he going crazy? No one else seemed to be going

through this. How could he spend so much time doing his schoolwork, yet never finish his papers on time?

Justin's sleeping and eating habits began to change. Nothing tasted good, and he didn't like going to the cafeteria anyway. So he retreated to his room even more. Soon he panicked too much to go to his classes. He was too depressed to do anything.

Justin was *not* crazy. He was going through what a lot of people call the "freshman crazies." It happens to a lot of people who go away to school for the first time—no matter how independent they are.

It is difficult for anyone to adjust to any new lifestyle or major changes. Many graduates beginning their careers go through the same thing. But if it happens to you the first time you get away from home, the worst thing you can do is dig yourself into a hole of depression. The deeper you dig and the longer you put off getting help, the harder it will be to get out.

How could Justin get out of his mess? He could ask around about a Christian counselor. That might be a difficult step to take, but it would be profitable in the end. He could get more involved in a college group at his church. He could also talk to one of his pastors, or even go to a resident assistant in his dormitory and ask for help. He could talk to another freshman who feels the same. (You'd be surprised how many freshmen go through this in the first semester of college.)

Whether you are on a Christian campus or not, please understand that you are not a "bad Christian" if you have problems adjusting to college. It is natural and help is available! Reach out; I know it is hard, but it is not impossible.

One more thing. Please understand that sometimes you can't pray this kind of problem away. Prayer helps you learn to give your will to God, but why would you pray for God to get you out of a hole that *you* seem to be digging deeper? If you have a ruptured appendix, you need to go to a doctor as well as pray. So please do not feel ashamed or weak if you feel like you need help for an emotional need.

**Turn to me and be gracious to me,
  for I am lonely and afflicted.
The troubles of my heart have multiplied;
  free me from my anguish.**

Psalm 25:16–17 (NIV)

49

The Real Israel

*F*inally, I was there. The beautiful land of Israel where everything I had read about in the Bible had taken place. I looked at all the people with foreign clothes on. Everything was so different . . . the looks in people's eyes, the smell of the passing bodies, the guttural sounds of their Hebrew language.

I did not think I had come with many expectations. I had studied about Israel the first semester of my freshman year of college, but I still had only a vague idea of what it would be like. The only images I had in my mind were biblical ones.

Our first day was absolutely beautiful! We were standing on a hill overlooking Bethlehem when a double rainbow appeared. I had never seen two rainbows in my life. Somehow it seemed like God was reassuring me that He was traveling in this foreign place with me. After that, however, feelings of disappointment started to set in.

Somehow my experience in Israel was not what I expected. I had expected the Holy Land to make me holier. I had expected the place where the Messiah walked to strengthen my faith. And I had expected the modern land of Israel to match the biblical images in my mind. I think I wanted the twelve disciples to come up and greet me by name! I wanted

to see Jesus beside an empty tomb. I wanted to see forty camels at a well waiting to be watered.

I did *not* want to see forty people coming up to me and asking me to buy stamps, wood, and other trinkets. I did not want to hear things like, "Well, they thought this was the place where Jesus was crucified, but there are two other places where it my have happened . . . ," or "Here is a rock left from Jesus' tomb . . . ," or "Look at this empty field; this might be where Jesus' disciples picked up corn on the Sabbath."

I was so frustrated! I could go to some field in Missouri and see the same thing!

It was truly awesome to see and walk through many of the real places that I have read about in the Bible. But even some of those weren't what I expected. It was like the time I was a small child and found out on vacation that there weren't thick black lines separating different states from each other . . . that you could be in Texas one second and Oklahoma the next and never know the difference if the sign weren't there. I guess I expected to be able to recognize everything and simply have a beautifully illustrated version of the Bible "boxed up" in my mind forever.

Aren't a lot of things like that for you? (They are for me.) Sometimes we think that life is going to be wrapped up in a beautiful package, then everything gets ripped to shreds. Parents divorce, somebody dies, a riot tears through a city, a lover leaves, a house burns down. We may get suckered into a terrible deal on a car or stuck in a class where the professor teaches the same fourteen-year-old lesson every year.

Life is rarely picture perfect. Plenty of experiences will shatter our images and expectations. (I can't wait to discover how difficult marriage is going to be!) In this life there are going to be greedy shopkeepers, scam artists, disloyal friends, and disappointments in every area of life.

We are not hopeless, though. God is big enough to handle

our disappointments. And although I don't think we need to go around complaining about everything, it is okay to feel disappointed with things at times.

I find that once I write my disappointments or talk about them with God, I usually gain a clearer perspective. I see that I was either expecting too much or I that I was really (legitimately) taken advantage of. In either case I need to learn how to draw on God's grace and wisdom.

It's not just other people and events that disappoint me, of course. I let myself down all the time. When that happens, I have to keep reminding myself that God loves me and forgives me where I am. I can then learn to forgive people—or even places and events—that let me down. Once I learned to forgive the disappointing parts of Israel, for instance, I quickly learned to enjoy all of the beautiful and great things about it. (If you get a chance, please go!)

I guess what I learned in all of this is to enjoy the good parts in life, to work through the negative times, and to expect to be disappointed from time to time. Our world used to be wrapped in a perfect package, but Adam and Eve opened it to a world of evil and sin. We cannot expect things to be perfect, and we cannot expect ourselves to be either. But we have hope anyway because, even in our weakness, God is strong! He'll never disappoint us.

My grace is sufficient for you, for My strength is made perfect in weakness.

2 Corinthians 12:9

About the Author

Cheryl Meier was seventeen when she began writing *I Know Just How You Feel.* The daughter of well-known Christian psychologist Paul Meier, she wrote this devotional for teenagers who want to know a God who will meet them where they are and accept them, with all their strengths and weaknesses.

In high school Cheryl was a cheerleader and an avid gymnast; since college she has taken up skateboarding and snowboarding. She is now studying psychology in southern California. This is her first book.